Peace Terms

DAN SNODDERLY, Editor

Peace Terms

GLOSSARY OF TERMS FOR CONFLICT MANAGEMENT AND PEACEBUILDING

SECOND EDITION

UNITED STATES INSTITUTE OF PEACE PRESS
Washington, DC

United States Institute of Peace Press
2301 Constitution Avenue, NW
Washington, DC 20037
www.usip.org

The paper used in this book meets the minimum requirements of American National Standards for Information Science—Permanence of Paper for Printed Library Materials, ANSI Z39.48-1984.

First edition published 2011.

Printed in the United States of America

Library of Congress Cataloging-in-Publication Data

Names: Snodderly, Daniel R., 1946- editor. | United States Institute of Peace, issuing body.
Title: Peace terms : glossary of terms for conflict management and peacebuilding / Dan Snodderly, editor.
Description: Second edition. | Washington, DC : United States Institute of Peace Press, [2018] |
Includes bibliographical references and index.
Identifiers: LCCN 2018000522 | ISBN 9781601276995 (alk. paper)
Subjects: LCSH: Peace-building--Dictionaries. | Conflict management--Dictionaries.
Classification: LCC JZ5533 .P43 2018 | DDC 303.6/603--dc23
LC record available at https://lccn.loc.gov/2018000522

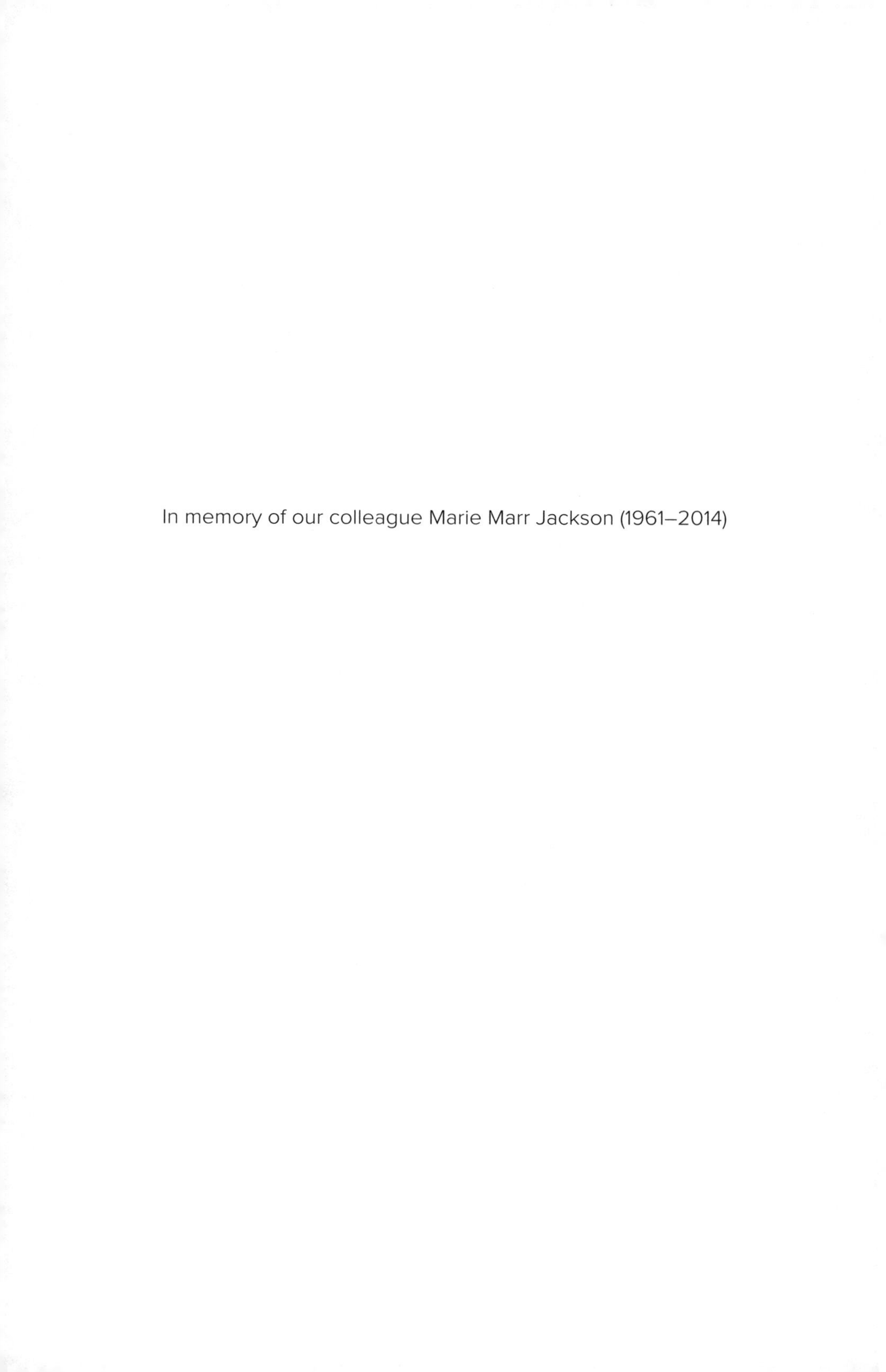

In memory of our colleague Marie Marr Jackson (1961–2014)

CONTENTS

FOREWORD

"To jaw-jaw is always better than to war-war."
—Winston Churchill

Communication is vital for building peace, and the ability to reach for words that connect rather than divide depends on a shared understanding. Yet the language of peacebuilding is not always clear in a rapidly changing world filled with specialized sectors, evolving vocabularies, and contested concepts.

The meanings of terms such as diplomacy, mediation, and negotiation are relatively straightforward. But what is the difference between autonomy and sovereignty? And how is peacekeeping different from peacemaking or peacebuilding?

To help answer these questions, the United States Institute of Peace published the first edition of *Peace Terms* in 2011. Since then, the glossary has been embraced by thousands of readers, bringing a shared understanding across the diverse fields of development, security, international relations, and peacebuilding.

The first edition of the glossary has been used by a wide audience—from peacebuilding practitioners and scholars to college students, from experienced professionals participating in USIP's Academy courses and trainings to high school students taking on their first research projects.

Much has changed since *Peace Terms* was first published. For this edition, we have added some sixty new terms—including such entries as customary justice, just peace theory, radicalization, resilience, and violent extremism—and we have substantially revised another fifteen—such as cyberattack, environmental security, human security, and violence—for a total of 350 terms.

An important new feature is the addition of boxed texts throughout the book, which allows us to explore in greater depth the more complex and confusing terms such as civil society, countering violent extremism, resilience, and tracks of diplomacy.

In developing this glossary, we realized that we needed to reach broad agreement on terminology, especially given the cross-disciplinary nature of the field. Accordingly, the editor, Dan Snodderly, has consulted a wide range of sources, as well as the entire senior staff and many others within and outside the USIP community.

Similarly, the definitions in this glossary have been drawn from many sources, not least of which are the Institute's own publications. Notable among these are the volumes by Chester A. Crocker, Fen Osler Hampson, and Pamela Aall—*Managing Conflict in a World Adrift* and *Herding Cats: Multiparty Mediation in a Complex World*—and the second edition of Chas. W. Freeman, Jr.'s *Diplomat's Dictionary*.

This edition of *Peace Terms* has been produced by USIP's Center for Applied Conflict Transformation (ACT), which is the hub of the Institute's thematic programs. The center leads the Institute's long-standing engagements on justice, security, and rule of law; inclusive societies; and current challenges to peace such as election violence and violent extremism. Among its many other functions, ACT designs and pilots tools for peacebuilders, such as the Global Campus's online courses and this glossary.

As was true of the first edition, this glossary is a living document. *Peace Terms* is by no means the last word, and we welcome feedback from aspiring, emerging, and seasoned peacebuilders alike as we continue to refine this compendium.

Nancy Lindborg, President
United States Institute of Peace

PREFACE

When the first edition of *Peace Terms* was published in 2011, I noted our need to reach broad agreement on the terminology of peacebuilding, especially given the cross-disciplinary nature of the field. As the field has evolved and expanded, that need has only expanded—hence this new, larger edition.

As with the first edition, I consulted a wide range of sources and individuals. Because this volume is intended for a broad audience, I did not footnote the text but instead listed the major sources at the end of the book. As before, I found that there were few agreed-upon definitions. Accordingly, definitions are sometimes original, sometimes composites of existing definitions, and sometimes existing definitions that I tightened or reframed. To highlight some of the most complicated terms, I have placed them in boxes spread throughout the text. Note also that the list of abbreviations includes many items that do not appear in the main text but could be useful to readers.

Fortunately, throughout this lengthy process I have had the support of many colleagues. I want to thank USIP senior staff for their thoughtful and constructive comments on the draft definitions, and especially Institute President Nancy Lindborg, Executive Vice President Bill Taylor, and ACT Vice President Carla Koppell for their encouragement and advice.

Also invaluable has been the support of Pamela Aall, Viola Gienger, Kay Spencer, and the talented and hardworking USIP publications team—Jake Harris, Cecilia Stoute, Peggy Archambault (who did the wonderful cover design), Delsena Draper (who did the equally wonderful interior design), Erica Sanford, and Jodi Narde. I also want to acknowledge the thoughtful and constructive comments by Matt Levinger and two anonymous reviewers. It was truly an ensemble performance. The book is stronger for everyone's involvement, but does not necessarily reflect their views.

Dan Snodderly

Accountability—The notion that individuals, including public officials, should be held responsible for their actions. ***Political accountability*** means the responsibility or obligation of government officials to act in the best interests of society or face consequences. ***Legal accountability*** concerns the mechanisms by which public officials can be held liable for actions that go against established rules and principles. In cases of crimes against humanity, accountability means that individuals should be held accountable by the state the crimes occurred in or by the international community.

Active listening—A way of listening that focuses on both the content of statements or responses in a dialogue and the underlying emotions. It means asking open-ended questions, seeking clarification, asking for specificity, and confirming your understanding of what the other party has said.

Adjudication—In international relations, adjudication involves the referral of a dispute to an impartial third-party tribunal, normally either an international court or an arbitration tribunal, for a binding decision. However, the state or states concerned must give their consent to participate either through special agreement or existing treaty. Because referral involves a permanent judicial body, the method for selecting judges and procedures of the court are already established. The best-known such court is probably the International Court of Justice. For more on referral to an arbitration tribunal, *see* Arbitration.

Advising—Foreign assistance in which technical experts share their expertise to address institutional or operational fragility of a process, system, or institution in a host country. Often embedded with counterparts in the office they advise, advisers are typically seasoned practitioners in such fields as logistics management, human resources, gender mainstreaming, contracting, and procurement.

Alliance—In international relations, a formal agreement among states to further common interests on security issues, often confirmed by treaty, for example, NATO.

Alternative dispute resolution (ADR)—In general, an approach to the resolution of conflicts that does not involve litigation and seeks an outcome at least minimally satisfactory to all parties concerned. It typically involves a third-party mediator or arbitrator. ADR tends to involve greater direct negotiation on the part of disputants than does litigation, takes much less time and money when successful, and seeks consensus. Many analysts no longer include the word "alternative." Others use ***appropriate dispute resolution***.

Amnesty—The setting aside or forgoing of punishment for specific offenses, often political. It usually applies to a group or class of people. Sometimes used as a synonym for pardon, but the latter usually refers to someone who has been convicted. Sometimes included in peace agreements to secure buy-in from combatants, but this practice is controversial because it can prevent accountability for war crimes and crimes against humanity.

Andragogy—*See* Pedagogy.

Appeasement—Traditionally, it simply meant making concessions to an aggressive power to prevent further conflict, but now typically used in a derogatory manner in reference to the Munich agreement of 1938 that allowed Germany to annex part of Czechoslovakia.

Arab League—Formally the League of Arab States (LAS), but usually referred to as the Arab League. It is a regional organization of more than twenty Arab countries in northern and northeastern Africa and southwestern Asia.

Arbitration—A form of international adjudication that involves the referral of a dispute or disputes to an ad hoc tribunal, rather than to a permanently established court, for binding decision. By agreement, the parties define the issues to be arbitrated, the method for selecting arbitrators, and the procedures for the tribunal. Because the parties have committed in advance (often by treaty) to accept the results, most states comply with arbitral awards. Perhaps the best-known recent example of conflict-related arbitration concerned control of the Brčko area, in Bosnia and Herzegovina, as part of the Dayton Peace Agreement. Arbitration differs from mediation, in which a third party helps the disputants develop a solution on their own. *See also* Adjudication *and* Mediation.

Armistice—An agreement to stop fighting pending a more formal settlement such as a treaty. Sometimes used as a synonym for truce or cease-fire, but these are generally more limited and may precede an armistice. In some cases, such as the Korean War, an armistice can become the status quo if no formal treaty is signed. *See also* Cease-fire *and* Treaty.

Arms control—A process of cooperation among states aimed at reducing the likelihood or scope of military action by adopting reciprocal measures to guard against surprise attack, to limit deployments, or to reduce armaments or the size and structure of armed forces.

Assessment—The wide variety of methods or tools used to evaluate, measure, and document a project or program. ***Baseline assessments*** establish a starting point for measuring progress over a period of time and provide a better understanding of the context for a project. ***Formative assessments*** can be made several times during this period and give program managers opportunities to modify the project in process. ***Endline or summative assessments*** are made at the end of the period and typically judge the overall success of the project. Common methods include interviews, focus groups, and surveys of participants, funders, and any other stakeholders in the project including recipients of its intended benefits. *See also* Needs assessment.

Asymmetry—When one person or party in a relationship has more power or leverage than another, whether the power is political, economic, or military, or results from greater experience or knowledge. *See also* Leverage.

Atrocities—*See* Mass atrocities.

Autonomy—Literally meaning self-government, autonomy was traditionally considered synonymous with self-determination and sometimes with sovereignty. Today it more frequently refers to an arrangement whereby a region of a country is granted extensive self-governance or de facto self-rule. In many cases, the region has demanded independence but agreed to autonomy in certain sectors such as police or education. Regions with autonomous arrangements include Aceh, Indonesia; Basque Country, Spain; Jammu and Kashmir, India; Muslim Mindanao, Philippines; Republika Srpska, Bosnia and Herzegovina; and Zanzibar, Tanzania.

Back-channel negotiation—Communications carried out in secret, usually as part of or in preparation for a larger negotiation, so as to avoid public disclosure of especially sensitive matters.

Balance of power—In international relations, a situation in which no state or group of states has so much power that it can dictate to the others or ignore their interests. A good example is the agreement reached at the Congress of Vienna in 1815, which attempted to provide a long-term plan for peace in Europe after the Napoleonic Wars.

Bargaining—A type of negotiation in which two sides debate the terms of an agreement. The zone of possible agreement (ZOPA), or bargaining range, is the overlapping area between the two parties' positions within which an agreement can be reached. An effective negotiator may be able to expand this range.

BATNA (best alternative to a negotiated agreement)—The measure against which parties should judge the proposed terms of any mediated or negotiated agreement.

Battle deaths—Fatalities among soldiers and civilians that are a direct result of combat between warring parties. They do not include deaths from one-sided violence such as civilians killed by a government or formally organized group. *See also* War.

Brokering—Broadly speaking, the term means helping others reach agreements. In international relations, it usually refers to an independent third party. It is often used as a synonym for facilitation and mediation. *See also* Facilitation *and* Mediation.

Capacity—The ability of people, institutions, and societies to perform functions, solve problems, and set and achieve objectives. Originally applied to institutions, more recently to a wide range of stakeholders, including individuals. At the individual level, capacity refers to the knowledge and skills that people have acquired by study or experience. At the organizational level, it refers to management structures, processes, systems, and practices as well as an institution's relationships with other organizations and sectors including public, private, and community organizations. ***Absorptive capacity*** refers to the amount of new information or aid that a country or institution can effectively use.

Capacity building—Enabling people, organizations, and societies to develop, strengthen, and expand their abilities to meet their goals or fulfill their mandates. Capacity is strengthened by developing knowledge and skills that enhance individual and collective abilities to deliver services and carry out programs in a sustainable way. A long-term and continuous process that focuses on developing human resources, organizational strength, and legal structures, it involves all stakeholders including civil society. Related terms include ***capacity development*** and ***capacity strengthening***, which emphasizes the need to build upon existing capacity as much as possible.

Cease-fire—A suspension of armed conflict agreed to by both sides. It may be aimed at freezing the conflict in place, in which case it is often called a ***cessation of hostilities agreement***. Or it may be a formal cease-fire with more elaborate terms and provisions including external monitoring, often undertaken as part of a larger negotiated settlement. A cease-fire is sometimes referred to as a ***truce***. When marking the permanent end of war, it is referred to as an ***armistice***. Beyond an armistice, parties can enter into a ***disengagement*** or ***separation of forces agreement***, and ultimately to a ***treaty***. *See also* Disengagement *and* Treaty.

Chapters 6 and 7—The sections of the UN Charter that deal most directly with dispute resolution and peacekeeping. Chapter 6, "Pacific Settlement of Disputes," stipulates that parties to a dispute should use peaceful methods to resolve the dispute, such as negotiation and mediation. It authorizes the Security Council to issue recommendations, but they are generally considered advisory rather than binding. Chapter 7, "Action with Respect to Threats to the Peace, Breaches of the Peace, and Acts of Aggression," authorizes more forceful methods such as economic coercion and severance of diplomatic relations. Should those measures prove inadequate, the Security Council may then "take such action by air, sea, or land forces as may be necessary to maintain or restore international peace and security." Although the word "peacekeeping" does not appear in the UN Charter, all UN peace operations have been authorized under either chapter 6, which restricts peacekeepers to using force only in self-defense, or chapter 7, which permits more robust peace enforcement missions with a mandate for protection of civilians. The informal term ***chapter 6 and a half*** refers to traditional UN peacekeeping operations that fall between the two. *See also* Peace enforcement, Peacekeeping, *and* Peacemaking.

Child soldier—A child associated with the armed forces of the state or of an armed group, regardless of whether the child is armed or participates in combat. Often conscripted by coercion or manipulation to serve as a fighter or as a cook, porter, informant, etc. International agreements define a child as anyone under the age of eighteen.

Citizen diplomacy—The unofficial contacts between people of different countries, as differentiated from official contacts between governmental representatives. Citizen diplomacy includes exchanges of people (such as students); international religious, scientific, and cultural activities; and unofficial dialogues, discussions, or negotiations between citizens of opposing countries, which is usually referred to as ***track 2 diplomacy***. In the latter case, citizens in the United States may seek authorization from the federal government in order to comply with the Logan Act, which prohibits unauthorized US citizens from interfering in relations between the United States and foreign governments. *See also* Tracks of diplomacy.

Civic mobilization—*See* Nonviolent civic action.

Civil affairs units—The military forces trained and equipped to conduct civil affairs activities and to support civil-military operations. For the United Nations, civil affairs officers are usually deployed at the local level to facilitate implementation of peacekeeping mandates and work to strengthen social and civic conditions necessary for peace. They are often the primary interface between the mission and the local population. For the US Army, "Civil Affairs units work with civil authorities and civilian populations in the commander's area of operations to lessen the impact of military operations." Most US Army civil affairs personnel are reservists—lawyers, city managers, economists, veterinarians, teachers, and police officers whose expertise will be particularly useful in the field. The Marine Corps, Navy, and Air Force also have civil affairs units. The British and Dutch armies have civil affairs units as well. *See also* Civil-military cooperation.

Civil-military cooperation (CIMIC)—The collaborative relationships between civilian and military actors in a conflict environment. Civilian actors may include government officials, staff from international organizations, and representatives of nongovernmental organizations. Cooperation ranges from occasional informational meetings to comprehensive programs where civilian and military partners share planning and implementation. These efforts can be controversial, as the military may see civilians as unduly complicating their mission, and civilians—especially in the humanitarian field—may think that any association with the military will compromise their impartiality and threaten their personal safety. Most experts, however, see civilian-military cooperation as necessary to provide the security, knowledge, and skills needed to help transform a conflict into an enduring peace.

Civil society—A complex term that encompasses a wide array of nongovernmental groups including civic, educational, trade, labor, business, charitable, media, religious, recreational, cultural, and advocacy groups as well as informal associations and social movements. In theory, its institutional forms are distinct from those of the state, though in practice the boundaries may be blurred. A strong civil society can protect individuals and groups against intrusive government, serve a watchdog function, and positively influence government behavior. However, some civil society groups—including militias, mafias, and paramilitary groups—organize around uncivil values and thus can create and perpetuate discord and even violence. In addition, most groups have discrete agendas not always representative of a larger range of issues. Some definitions do not include commercial enterprises but do include business associations. Some do not consider the media, most of which is for profit, to be part of civil society, but rather a tool that can either promote or undermine civil society. A related term is ***civil society organization (CSO)***.

Civil war—A large-scale armed conflict within a country fought either for control of all or part of the state, for a greater share of political or economic power, or for the right to secede. Opinions on how to define "large-scale" differ, but some say that a conflict must cause at least a thousand war-related deaths per year to be considered a civil war.

Coercive diplomacy—The use of threats or limited force to persuade an opponent to refrain from, call off, or undo an action. It may seek to achieve either ***deterrence*** (employing threats to dissuade an opponent from undertaking an action that has not yet begun) or ***compellence*** (using threats or limited application of force such as sanctions to persuade an opponent to reverse an action it has already taken, for example to return territory it has invaded or give up its arsenal of nuclear weapons). Coercive diplomacy can be coupled with positive inducements, or "carrots."

Combatant—The members of the armed forces of a party to a conflict, not including medical and religious personnel. ***Noncombatant*** describes civilians, medics and chaplains, and sick or wounded combatants. ***Civilians*** are those who are not members of the armed forces. In the case of militias and other armed opposition groups, the line between civilians and combatants may be blurred.

Communication styles—Communication occurs in a range of styles in all cultures but can be broadly defined as either ***low context*** (individualistic) or ***high context*** (relationship-oriented). In low-context communication, meaning is explicit and indirectness is considered evasive and potentially dishonest. In high-context communication, the listener must figure out the implicit meaning at play, being sure to observe the nonverbal subtleties that enhance speech. Directness and confrontation are considered offensive and rude. It is often challenging for low-context professionals from countries like the United States to communicate effectively with counterparts from countries such as Japan, Egypt, or India who have more high-context styles of interaction.

Conciliation—Often used as a synonym for mediation, though it implies not only reaching a formal agreement but also reducing hostility and building trust. Mediation seems to be the more common term.

Confidence-building measure (CBM)—An agreement to exchange information about and allow monitoring of political and, more frequently, military activities in order to build trust and reduce the risk of conflict escalation. Some measures establish rules regarding the movement of military forces. CBMs typically rely on tools for maintaining direct and quick communication and monitoring among governments and military forces, such as hotlines, regularly scheduled exchange of information about military missions, and prenotification about troop exercises or missile tests. Some analysts use the broader term ***confidence- and security-building measure (CSBM).***

Conflict—An inevitable aspect of human interaction, conflict is present when two or more individuals or groups pursue mutually incompatible goals. Conflicts can be waged violently, as in a war, or nonviolently, as in an election or an adversarial legal process. When channeled constructively into processes of resolution, conflict can be beneficial. *See also* Violence *and* War.

Conflict analysis—The systematic study of conflict in general and of individual or group conflicts in particular. Conflict analysis provides a structured inquiry into the causes and potential trajectory of a conflict to better understand the processes of resolution. ***Conflict assessment*** and ***conflict mapping*** are sometimes used to describe the process of identifying stakeholders, their interests and positions, and the possibility for conflict management. A large number of analytical frameworks are available, including the US government's Interagency Conflict Assessment Framework (ICAF) and USAID's Conflict Assessment Framework.

Conflict curve—A conceptual tool that helps illustrate how conflicts tend to evolve over time and how different phases of conflict relate to one another, as well as how to identify kinds of third-party intervention (see figure 1). This knowledge helps practitioners determine effective strategies for intervention and the best timing of those strategies.

Figure 1. The Conflict Curve

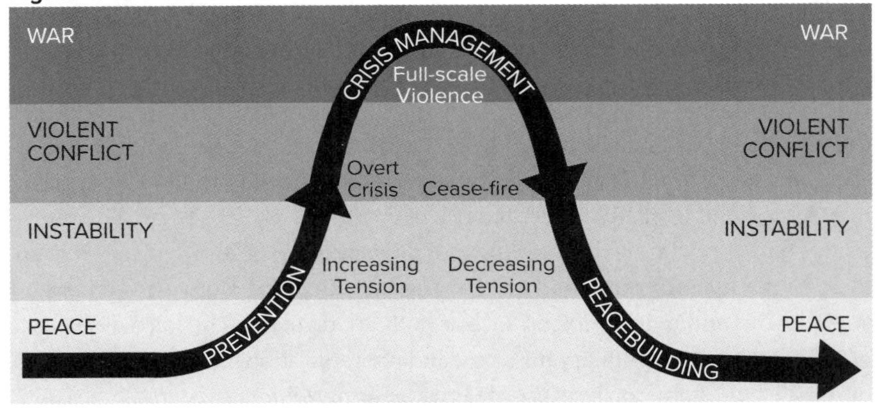

The vertical axis shows the intensity of conflict and levels of violence; the horizontal axis shows the duration of conflict over time. This is an oversimplified model, intended for illustrative purposes only; actual conflicts can exhibit many deviations from this curve.

Conflict entrepreneur—Any group or individual whose profits depend on conditions that promote conflict. Most often used to describe those who engage in or directly benefit from illegal economic activity that promotes violence or undermines efforts for good governance and economic development. These actors can exist inside or outside of government.

Conflict management—A general term that describes efforts to prevent, limit, contain, or resolve conflicts, especially violent ones, while building up the capacities of all parties involved to undertake peacebuilding. It is based on the concept that conflicts are a normal part of human interaction and are rarely completely resolved or eliminated, but can be managed by such measures as negotiation, mediation, conciliation, and arbitration. Conflict management also supports the longer-term development of societal systems and institutions that enhance good governance, rule of law, security, economic sustainability, and social well-being, which helps prevent future conflicts. ***Peacemaking*** is closely related but tends to focus on halting ongoing conflicts and reaching partial agreements or broader negotiated settlements. A similar term is ***conflict mitigation***. *See also* Peacemaking.

Conflict mitigation—*See* Conflict management.

Conflict prevention—This term is used most often to refer to measures taken to keep low-level or long-festering disputes from escalating into violence, but it can also apply to efforts to limit the spread of violence if it does occur or to avoid reoccurrence of violence. It may include official actions such as early-warning systems, confidence-building measures (hotlines, notification of troop movements), preventive deployment of peacekeeping forces, and sanctions, and such nonofficial efforts as youth engagement and grassroots intercommunity dialogue. *See also* Preventive diplomacy.

Conflict resolution—Efforts to address the underlying causes of a conflict by finding common interests and goals. It includes fostering positive attitudes and generating trust through reconciliation initiatives, and building or strengthening the institutions and processes through which the parties interact peacefully.

Conflict transformation—A recently developed concept that emphasizes addressing the structural roots of conflict by changing existing patterns of behavior and creating a culture of nonviolent approaches. It proposes an integrated approach to peacebuilding that aims to bring about long-term changes in personal, relational, structural, and cultural dimensions. Recognizing that societies in conflict have existing systems that still function, conflict transformation focuses on building up local institutions as well as reducing drivers of conflict.

Constabulary force—A specialized unit trained and equipped to operate in peace operations, providing police-type functions like crowd control in high-threat environments where traditional police tactics would be ineffective but the use of military forces would be too lethal. The unit is equipped in military fashion but operates as police. In some countries, constabulary units are permanent forces that deal with such high-violence situations as fighting the mafia or terrorism.

Constitution making—The drafting of a new constitution, especially when seen as a key element of democratization and state building. This process is crucial to outlining the vision of a new society, defining the fundamental principles by which a state will be organized, and distributing or redistributing political power. Moreover, the constitution-making process itself can be a vehicle for national dialogue and the consolidation of peace. The term ***constitution building*** is sometimes used to encompass the entire process of making and implementing a new constitution; it may include peace agreements, new laws and institutions, and civic education.

Constructive ambiguity—When negotiating parties cannot agree on an issue but paper over their disagreement by using ambiguous language. Negotiation can then proceed in the hope that the issue will be resolved later or cease to be a concern.

Constructive engagement—The theory that it is generally more productive for the international community to engage a country's leaders through quiet diplomacy than through such harsh measures as sanctions and divestment. Originally used by the Reagan administration in relation to the apartheid regime in South Africa. Recently applied more widely, including to business practices and environmental stakeholders.

Contact group—An ad hoc grouping of influential countries that have a significant interest in policy developments in a particular country or region, such as the Balkans or piracy off the coast of Somalia. The term is usually associated with some form of peace process or negotiation in which contact group members play a supportive role. *See also* Quartet.

Convention—*See* Treaty.

Corporate social responsibility—The notion that a business should take responsibility for the impact of its activities on its employees, customers, communities, and the environment. Perhaps the best-known international example is the violent dispute over control of oil production in Nigeria. Foreign companies have been accused not of committing violence but of benefiting from and doing little to stop government attacks against the protestors. Some analysts argue that expecting corporations to play this kind of role is unrealistic, and that it is properly the domain of government.

Corruption—The abuse of power for private gain, including bribery, extortion, fraud, nepotism, embezzlement, falsification of records, kickbacks, and influence peddling. Although commonly associated with the public sector, it is also found in the business and NGO sectors.

Countering violent extremism (CVE)—A contested term that has different meanings across US government agencies and internationally. It refers to a range of policy, programs, and interventions designed to prevent individuals from engaging in violence associated with radical political, social, cultural, and religious ideologies and groups, though it is mostly linked with terrorist groups. CVE emerged from and, for the most part, remains parked in the international and national security policymaking community as part of a broader effort to counter terrorism. However, the relevance and participation of development and peacebuilding organizations and approaches to the problem of violent extremism have led to a broader conceptualization and framing of this evolving field. *See also* Extremism, Radicalization, *and* Violent extremism.

Crimes against humanity—The mass killing of and targeted attacks against civilians, including systematic rape. These crimes are described more fully in the Rome Statute of the International Criminal Court, article 7. To be found guilty, an individual must have developed or carried out a policy of widespread or systematic violations. Crimes against humanity do not require the specific intent that genocide does "to destroy, in whole or in part, a national, ethnical, racial or religious group, as such." *See also* Genocide.

Crisis management—An attempt to control events during a crisis to prevent significant and systematic violence from occurring or escalating; usually involves finding a balance between coercion and accommodation.

Culture—The shared beliefs, traits, attitudes, behavior, products, and artifacts common to a particular social or ethnic group. ***Cross-cultural*** refers to interactions across cultures and reflects the fact that different cultures may have different communication styles and negotiating behavior. ***Multicultural*** refers to the acceptance of different ethnic cultures within a society. ***Cultural sensitivity*** means being aware of cultural differences and how they affect behavior, and moving beyond cultural biases and preconceptions to interact effectively. *See also* Communication styles.

Customary justice—A broad term used to denote community-based social regulation and dispute resolution practices that are distinct from, even if influenced by and intertwined with, the state-sponsored Western-style justice system. The term encompasses a vast array of practices that vary from community to community and does not imply a single, uniform system. Such practices, however, generally originate in long-standing localized social structures, which greatly inform their notions of justice. Other terms are often used interchangeably with customary justice; strictly speaking, they are usually not synonyms, however. These alternative terms include ***traditional law/justice, informal law/justice,*** and ***nonstate law/justice.*** In some countries, ***religious law*** may also overlap with, influence, or be conflated with customary legal orders. *See also* Dispute resolution *and* Justice.

Cyberattack—Any deliberate offensive action with the intent to disrupt, damage, destroy, steal, or gain unauthorized access to a computer system or network, from low-level vandalism to major efforts to disable a nation's infrastructure. ***Cybercampaign*** and ***cyberwarfare*** describe more prolonged and focused efforts. ***Cyberterrorism*** refers to politically motivated attacks intended to disrupt or intimidate a given population.

Declaration of principles—A negotiating framework that provides the overall structure for a subsequent detailed peace agreement. It usually contains the broad outlines of an agreement, stated in general terms and acceptable to the parties at the table, political leaders, and the general public.

Demilitarization—Prohibiting military forces in an area, often as part of a truce or peace treaty. It may also mean reducing or eliminating a state's armed forces. A ***demilitarized zone*** is typically a buffer zone between former combatants, as in Korea.

Demobilization—Reducing the size of a country's armed forces after a war. In an internal conflict, it also means disarming paramilitaries and insurgents. *See also* Disarmament, demobilization, and reintegration.

Democracy—A state or community in which all adult members of society partake in a free and fair electoral process that determines government leadership, have access to power through their representatives, and enjoy universally recognized freedoms and liberties. ***Democracy building*** or ***democratization*** is the exercise of consolidating and strengthening institutions that help support democratic government—institutions that may relate to rule of law initiatives, political party development, constitution building, public administration development, and civil society education programs.

Deterrence—An effort to persuade an opponent to not take an action because the costs and risks of doing so will outweigh what might be gained. *See also* Coercive diplomacy.

Developed and developing countries—There is no consensus on the standard for categorizing countries as developed or developing. In general, developed countries have a higher per capita income, and developing countries a lower per capita income and a less developed industrial base. Related terms include ***underdeveloped countries*** and ***least developed countries***.

Development—Generally, the process of improving people's lives. Originally, it focused on the goal of greater economic prosperity and opportunity. It now typically takes into account such issues as governance, education, the environment, and human rights.

Development aid—The assistance provided to developing countries to support their economic, social, and political development. It usually comes from individual countries or international organizations such as the UN Development Programme and the World Bank Group. Development aid tends to be aimed at long-term problems such as poverty, whereas ***humanitarian aid*** is usually aimed at short-term problems such as providing clean water or food. ***Tied aid*** refers to the practice by most donors of insisting that aid be spent on goods and services from the donor country. ***Conditional aid*** refers to assistance that comes with specific requirements that the recipient must meet, such as reducing corruption or fighting terrorism.

Dialogue—A sustained interaction among groups to learn from each other and transform relationships, as they address practical and structural issues in society. Dialogue processes involve structured face-to-face encounters in focused, facilitated groups with participants representing various stakeholders. Dialogues range in purpose from relationship building and increasing understanding to deliberation and action. Whether a ***community-based dialogue*** or a ***dialogue of elites***, the process is based on agreed-upon norms and rooted in deep listening in which participants are willing to be changed by what they hear. Dialogue processes involve the exploration of complex issues related to identity and conflict, community or national priorities, or contentious sociopolitical issues. *See also* Facilitation.

Diaspora—The movement, migration, or scattering of a people away from an established or ancestral homeland. Also, a group of such people.

Diplomacy—The fundamental means by which foreign policy is implemented. It is the management of international relations by peaceful means, rather than through warfare, though it may involve threats of force. Official or track 1 diplomacy is typically carried out by government officials, who use bargaining, negotiation, and other peaceful means to negotiate treaties, trade policies, and other international agreements, including agreements to prevent, limit, manage, or settle conflicts. Unofficial or nonofficial (also called track 2) diplomacy refers to the use of nontraditional diplomatic agents, including business executives, religious figures, nongovernmental organizations, academics, and other private citizens who are typically conducting dialogue and problem-solving activities. *See also* Citizen diplomacy, Preventive diplomacy, Public diplomacy, *and* Tracks of diplomacy.

Disappearances—A euphemism for politically motivated murders or abductions, usually performed by or with the support of government or political organizations. Disappearances have occurred in many countries, the best known examples probably being Nazi Germany and Argentina in the late 1970s and early 1980s.

Disarmament, demobilization, and reintegration (DDR)—The process of disarming soldiers or other fighters, disconnecting them from their military units or disbanding those units, and helping them integrate socially and economically into society by finding civilian livelihoods. This can be achieved by comprehensive programs offering skills training, job creation, housing, psychological assistance, and resocialization.

Disengagement—The act of gradually withdrawing military forces and perhaps also political influence from an area. It might include planning for an orderly hand-off to a UN force. The term can also apply to a policy of watchful nonintervention.

Displaced person—*See* Internally displaced person *and* Refugee.

Dispute resolution—Typically, a process for resolving differences between two or more parties or groups without involving a court. Sometimes referred to as alternative dispute resolution or appropriate dispute resolution. Mostly used for domestic issues, it may involve negotiation, mediation, arbitration, collaborative law, or—in some definitions—litigation. Sometimes used as a synonym for conflict resolution as it relates to domestic issues. *See also* Customary justice *and* Justice.

Do no harm—A maxim acknowledging that any intervention entails a risk of doing harm, and that practitioners should proceed with programs only after careful consideration and widespread consultation. In assistance activities, the maxim recognizes that resources inevitably represent the distribution of power and wealth and will create tensions if careful attention is not given to how they are distributed and delivered.

Donor coordination—Efforts to integrate the work of donors, the host government, and local nongovernmental organizations so as to avoid duplication and inefficiencies.

Donor fatigue—Decreased support for aid and direct interventions in conflict-affected states in response to a perception that these efforts have not produced their expected results.

Early warning—An assessment and report of a high-risk situation to provide timely notice of escalating violence. Early-warning systems have been used to assess environmental threats, the risk of nuclear accident, natural disasters, mass movements of populations, the threat of famine, and the spread of disease, as well as violent conflict.

Education—The process of imparting or acquiring knowledge, skills, and values and developing the powers of reasoning and judgment, whether at an educational institution or independently. The line between education and training can be fuzzy, and many writers refer to ***education and training (E&T)*** as a single term. *See also* Peace (and conflict) studies, Pedagogy, *and* Training.

Elections—The process by which citizens typically choose representatives to the legislative and sometimes executive and judiciary branches. Voting systems vary widely, but most are either proportional or majoritarian. It is important to note that holding elections is only one part of democracy building.

Eminent persons—A group of distinguished and well-respected individuals typically gathered for a specific task, such as the Panel of Eminent Persons on United Nations–Civil Society Relations, the Organization for Security and Co-operation in Europe Panel of Eminent Persons asked to draw up a new vision for OSCE, and the Association of Southeast Asian Nations Eminent Persons Group tasked to create a charter for ASEAN.

Environmental security—A relatively new field that focuses on the connections among the environment, resources, security, conflict, and peacebuilding. Environmental changes that can negatively affect national security include depletion of fresh water supplies, depletion of fisheries, degradation of biodiversity, degradation of agricultural lands, food and health safety, ozone depletion, and climate change. Although the link between violent conflict and scarcity has been much debated, it seems clear that fighting over scarce resources can cause further conflict. But it is also clear that joint efforts to protect the environment across national borders can contribute to peacebuilding, as has been the case in various forms of cross-border water cooperation.

Escalation—An increase in intensity or scope of a conflict. The number of parties tends to increase, as does the number and breadth of the issues. ***De-escalation*** is the lessening of the intensity of a conflict as parties tire out or begin to realize that the conflict is doing them more harm than good, or as conflict management efforts begin to take effect. It can create space for more intensive efforts to resolve the conflict.

Ethics—The principles of conduct (right and wrong behavior) governing an individual or a group.

Ethnic cleansing—The deliberate, organized, and usually violent expulsion of people from an area on the basis of their perceived ethnic, communal, sectarian, or religious identity.

Evaluation—The systematic collection and analysis of data on a program, both as to the process and outputs (materials and activities) and the impact or outcome (immediate and longer term effects). *See also* Metrics, Monitoring, Outcomes, *and* Outputs.

Extremism—A complex phenomenon, extremism refers to views or measures that are at the far end of a political, social, or religious spectrum. It is synonymous with radicalism and is typically used to express disapproval. It does not necessarily imply the embrace of violence. At times, it is applied by Western and non-Western governments to describe Islamic political movements, although extremist movements exist in many, if not most, countries. *See also* Countering violent extremism, Radicalization, *and* Violent extremism.

Facilitation—The process or set of skills by which a third party attempts to help disputants move toward resolution of a dispute. It can operate at many levels, from providing good offices to a more active role as a mediator. It may mean helping the parties set ground rules and agendas for meetings, helping with communication between the parties, and analysis of the situation and possible outcomes—in general, helping the participants keep on track and working toward mutual goals. It may also mean helping set those goals. *See also* Dialogue *and* Mediation.

Fact finding—An investigation of a dispute by an impartial third party that examines the issues and facts in the case and may issue a report and recommended settlement, such as the Independent International Fact-Finding Mission on the Conflict in Georgia established by the Council of the European Union. A related term is ***commission of inquiry***, as in the International Commission of Inquiry on Darfur established by the United Nations.

Federalism—A system of governance characterized by two or more levels, each directly elected by its citizens and constitutionally empowered with legislative authority sufficient to achieve a degree of genuine autonomy. It is a power-sharing arrangement especially favored by large, culturally diverse countries such as India, Nigeria, the United States, and the former Yugoslavia. *See also* Autonomy *and* Power sharing.

Foreign aid—The economic and technical assistance used as instruments of policy to achieve certain goals. There are three main types of foreign aid—humanitarian, military, and development. Aid may be bilateral or multilateral, the latter usually being channeled through an international body.

Fragility—The absence or breakdown of a social contract between people and their government. Fragile states suffer from deficits of institutional capacity and political legitimacy that increase the risk of instability and violent conflict and sap the state of its resilience to disruptive shocks.

Gacaca—The Rwandan government's community-based judicial process, established in 2001 to help deal with the massive number of detainees accused of committing crimes against humanity during the 1994 genocide. These courts were closed in 2009.

Game theory—The study of mathematical models of negotiation, conflict, and cooperation between individuals, organizations, and governments. The value of game theory in negotiations, for example, is that it helps people understand the calculations the other side makes when that side has incomplete information. *See also* Win-win versus zero-sum.

Gender-based violence—Violence directed against individuals or groups on the basis of gender or sex. It includes acts or threats of acts that inflict physical or mental harm or suffering, coercion, and other deprivations of liberty, including rape, torture, mutilation, sexual slavery, forced impregnation, and murder. Although men and boys can be victims of gender-based violence, women and girls are the primary victims. *See also* Gender sensitivity *and* Sexual violence.

Gender sensitivity—The ability to recognize gender issues, especially women's different perspectives and interests arising from their different social situations and gender roles. Gender sensitivity is considered the beginning stage of gender awareness, leading to efforts to address gender-related impacts of conflict and peacebuilding. *See also* Gender-based violence *and* Sexual violence.

Geneva Conventions—The four treaties, with subsequent additions and revisions, that set the widely accepted legal standards for humane treatment of noncombatants (medical and religious personnel and civilians) and combatants who are no longer able to fight, including the sick, wounded, and prisoners of war. The first convention was adopted in 1864 and the fourth in 1949; the most recent protocol was added in 2005.

Genocide—Defined by the UN Convention on the Prevention and Punishment of the Crime of Genocide as "any of a number of acts committed with the intent to destroy, in whole or in part, a national, ethnical, racial, or religious group: killing members of the group; causing serious bodily or mental harm to members of the group; deliberately inflicting on the group conditions of life calculated to bring about its physical destruction in whole or in part; imposing measures intended to prevent births within the group; and forcibly transferring children of the group to another group." Some analysts use the term ***cultural genocide*** to refer to the destruction of cultural heritage, such as books, artworks, and structures, and the suppression of cultural activities. *See also* Holocaust.

Good offices—Typically, low-key actions by a third party to bring opposing parties to dialogue or negotiation. May include informal consultations to facilitate communication; offer of transportation, security, or site of venue; or fact finding. The third party may suggest ways into negotiations and a settlement but usually stops short of participation in negotiations. Norway's role in the 1993 Oslo Accords concerning the Israeli-Palestinian conflict is a classic example. ***Mediation*** and ***conciliation*** tend to be more active roles.

Governance—The exercise of authority to implement rules and policies in an effort to bring order to the social, political, economic, and judicial processes that allow a society to develop. ***Good governance*** involves a process that is informed and to a degree monitored by, and ultimately serves, all members of society. It also implies a level of accountability and transparency, both of which help ameliorate the risk of corruption and its corrosive and destabilizing impact.

Guarantor—A state, group of states, international organization, alliance, or other entity that ensures an agreement, in some cases by force. Originally it referred to a formal, legal commitment to take action in the event of a breach of obligations by a party to a treaty. In recent years, the term has been used more loosely to refer to a party that monitors or bears witness to an accord.

Guerrilla war—Warfare conducted by an irregular military or paramilitary unit using techniques such as harassment, sabotage, and surprise attacks against a more powerful force. Guerrilla groups may seize control of and live among unarmed civilian populations that provide labor, food, and other supplies, sometimes under duress. Successful guerrilla campaigns are usually protracted and have the support of the local population as well as external assistance.

Hate speech—Speech that is intended to foster hatred against groups based on race, religion, gender, sexual preference, national origin, or other traits. At the least it fosters hatred and discrimination, and at its worst it promotes violence and killing.

Holocaust—When capitalized, the term refers specifically to the genocide of European Jews and others by Nazi Germany and its collaborators during the 1930s and 1940s. *See also* Genocide.

Host country ownership—*See* Local ownership.

Human capital—The stock of knowledge and skill embodied in the population of an economy. It can be increased through investments in education, health care, and job training. ***Social capital*** comprises the resources that create a strong network of institutionalized relationships in society, which in turn facilitates civic engagement and encourages bargaining, compromise, and pluralistic politics, and contributes to economic and social development.

Humanitarian aid/assistance—Traditionally associated with natural disasters such as floods, fires, and famines, but more recently applied to social or political unrest, usually with the consent of the host country. It can include providing food, shelter, clothing, and medicine and medical personnel; evacuating the most vulnerable; and restoring basic amenities (water, sewage, power supplies). Aid can be given during the emergency itself and in the rehabilitation phase.

Humanitarian intervention—Action taken to protect unarmed civilian populations at risk. Some analysts use the term interchangeably with "military intervention"; others argue it should be reserved for delivery of humanitarian aid. Broadly speaking, the term includes nonmilitary as well as military interventions. *See also* International humanitarian law.

Human rights—The basic prerogatives and freedoms to which every person is entitled. Supported by the United Nation's Universal Declaration of Human Rights of 1948 and several international agreements, these rights include life, liberty, education, equality before law, association, belief, free speech, religion, and movement. Some argue that economic, social, and cultural rights should be included.

Human security—A relatively new concept that emphasizes the individual's need for freedom from fear and freedom from want, as well as specific needs such as food, health, and environmental security. Some analysts argue that the term is too vague and expansive to be useful, while others counter that it should be even more encompassing and include military security. *See also* Security.

I

Identity—The way people see themselves, that is, the qualities of a person or group that they feel make them different from others. Some theorists distinguish between collective identity, social identity, and personal identity. ***Identity conflicts*** develop when a person or group feels that their sense of self is threatened or denied legitimacy or respect. ***Identity politics*** exploits such conflicts for political advantage.

Ideology—A system of beliefs or theories, usually about politics or culture, held by an individual or a group.

Illicit networks—The people involved in such crimes as trafficking (drug, arms, and human), terrorism, kidnapping, counterfeiting goods or currency, and organ harvesting. Rapid developments in information technology, including social networking, have provided increased opportunities for these activities by organized crime, transnational terrorists, and other nonstate actors, and these networks can provide funding and logistical support for terrorism and other national security threats.

Impartiality—Regarding foreign aid, impartiality means assistance must be based on need alone, without regard to nationality, race, religion, class, or politics; it does not imply equal provision of aid. In mediation or peacekeeping, impartiality means treating the contending sides equitably and with fairness. *See also* Neutrality.

Incentives and disincentives—Efforts to persuade another person or group to undertake a desired action and thus avoid conflict. Incentives include foreign aid, visits by foreign leaders, security assurances, membership in international organizations, and removal of existing penalties. Disincentives include sanctions, boycotts, embargoes, and blockades. *See also* Sanctions.

Inclusive peace processes—The processes that provide diverse members of society the opportunity to be informed and consulted and to have their concerns better addressed before, during, and after formal peace agreements, resulting in more sustainable peace. Providing everyone—especially those most affected by violence—the chance to influence the decision-making process and be actively engaged in their country's transformation enables tensions to be more effectively resolved and strengthens legitimacy in the outcomes.

Indicator (of outcomes)—A measurable change that represents achievement of an outcome, typically those related to a program's goals. *See also* Evaluation, Outcomes, *and* Outputs.

Individualism versus collectivism—Broadly speaking, individualism refers to societies that stress individual identity over group identity. It is associated with values like self-sufficiency, individual responsibilities, and personal autonomy. Collectivism refers to societies that tend to emphasize "we" over "I"; group rights predominate over individual rights and group needs over individual wants and desires.

Informal economy—The exchange of goods and services that is usually neither taxed nor regulated by the government. It may be done through barter or sale, and may include such activities as day care, tutoring, and street trading as well as illegal or black market exchanges. Also referred to as the ***parallel***, ***shadow***, or ***underground economy***.

Information and communication technologies (ICTs)—A diverse set of tools used to create, disseminate, and manage information. These rapidly evolving technologies include the internet, intranets, wireless networks, cell phones, videoconferencing, and distance learning. The new ICTs have led to a new vocabulary that includes terms such as ***blogosphere*** (the connected community of blogs), ***citizen journalism*** (nonprofessionals creating their own media to report and disseminate the news), ***crowdsourcing*** (outsourcing a task to a group of people through a collaborative open call), and ***social media platforms*** (including participatory mapping projects like Ushahidi).

Infrastructure—The system of public works of a country, state, or region, including buildings and equipment to support highways, airports, and facilities for waste treatment and water supply, electricity, and communications. Some analysts use the term more broadly to include political and socioeconomic aspects.

Instability—A situation in which the parties perceive one another as enemies and maintain deterrent military capabilities but do not deploy armed force. The threat of violence is absent or only sporadic. A balance of power may discourage aggression, but crisis and war are still possible.

Insurgency—Paramilitary, guerrilla, or other uprising directed against a state from within to achieve political objectives. Typically aims to either replace the current regime or to secede from the state. Successful efforts have the support of the local population. ***Counterinsurgency*** efforts therefore seek to separate the insurgents from the population by winning their "hearts and minds," most often by undertaking badly needed reforms.

Interests—*See* Positions versus interests.

Interfaith dialogue—Efforts to promote understanding of and cooperation among faiths, especially as a tool to advance peacemaking and peacebuilding.

Internally displaced person (IDP)—Anyone forced to leave their home, in particular as a result of armed conflict, generalized violence, violations of human rights, or natural or human-made disasters, but who has not crossed an internationally recognized state border. *See also* Refugee.

International community—Literally, the term means all the countries of the world, or at least its major political leaders and organizations. Implies a consensus on specific issues such as human rights, but some critics charge that it mostly is used to refer to Western views. Examples include the United Nations, International Criminal Court, International Civil Aviation Organization, and various groupings of NGOs that provide relief during natural disasters. The term should not be seen, however, as synonymous with world government or global governance, which imply a sovereign power over states.

International financial institutions (IFI)—The international and regional development banks such as the World Bank Group and the African Development Bank, as well as the International Monetary Fund (IMF), which focuses primarily on trade and currency issues that threaten financial stability. A related term is ***Bretton Woods institutions***, named after the 1944 conference that established the World Bank and the IMF.

International humanitarian law (IHL)—The law of war outlined in the Geneva Conventions, the Hague Conventions, and customary international law, and supported by other documents. Defines the conduct and responsibilities of nations and individuals engaged in warfare, especially as relates to the protection of civilians. Generally applicable to international conflicts. A small subset apply to internal conflicts.

International organization (IO) or intergovernmental organization (IGO)—A formal institutional structure generally created by international agreement to foster cooperation in specific areas. In the conflict management field, the primary international organization is the United Nations, though regional organizations such as the Organization for Security and Co-operation in Europe, the Organization of American States, and the Association of Southeast Asian Nations play an increasingly active role.

Intervention—The involvement by a third party or parties in the internal affairs of a country. It may be military or nonmilitary, requested or imposed. Traditionally, nonintervention was the norm, but recently the international community has become more willing to act to alleviate widespread human suffering when the state is unwilling or unable to address such conditions. Other examples of coercive actions include punishing aggression by one state against another, enforcing violations of international agreements, and preventing an impending ecological catastrophe. *See also* Protection of civilians *and* Responsibility to protect.

Intractable conflict—A conflict that continues for a long time, resisting attempts to resolve it. Typically involves fundamental value disagreements, high-stakes distributional questions, domination issues, and denied human needs—usually the most difficult kinds of problems.

Justice—At a minimum, fair and equal treatment before the law—a system of rule of law based on legal procedures that apply to all members of society. ***Social justice*** refers to a situation characterized by rule of law and fair distribution of resources and opportunities in society. Some see justice as a prerequisite for a stable and lasting order; others argue that there can be no justice without order. ***Access to justice*** refers to efforts to make the justice system accessible to those who are otherwise excluded. ***Nonstate justice***, also called ***customary*** or ***traditional justice***, refers to the settlement of disputes outside the formal state justice system, for example through tribal and community councils. Such mechanisms are widely used in rural and poor urban areas but sometimes reinforce local inequities and social exclusion, especially concerning women. *See also* Restorative justice.

Just peace theory—A relatively recent concept developed as an alternative to just war theory. It includes practices such as supporting nonviolent direct action; cooperative conflict resolution; advancing democracy, human rights, and religious liberty; fostering just and sustainable economic development; and encouraging grassroots peacemaking groups and voluntary associations. *See also* Just war theory.

Just war theory—The belief that use of military force is acceptable only if it meets certain standards: right authority, just cause, right intention, last resort, proportional means, and reasonable prospects of success. The actual conduct of the war must meet the standards of proportional means and discrimination (immunity for noncombatants). Different sources cite somewhat different standards. *See also* Just peace theory.

Knowledge transfer—Sharing information and skills with a target audience and enabling them to integrate that knowledge into their daily practice. Full integration occurs when they can pass the knowledge along to others. Knowledge transfer can be accomplished by such methods as education, training, mentoring, advising, and shadowing.

Legitimacy—In international relations, the term generally refers to a government's right to govern based on the consent of the governed, a consent secured through elections, judicial controls, laws, and other checks and balances. More specifically, in an intervention, legitimacy refers to the degree to which the operation is authorized by an appropriate international or regional body, and the operation's mandate and conduct are accepted or at least tolerated by the affected population and the host country government.

Leverage—The power that one party has to influence the behavior of another party. It can come from many sources, such as being able to wait longer or having something the other party wants or needs. Leverage can be increased by facilitation, communication (providing translation or intelligence), or manipulation (reframing, rearranging, relocating).

Liberalism—A school of thought that argues that peace can best be achieved by the spread of democracy, freedom and equality, a market economy, the rule of law, and collective security. Traditionally, liberalism focused on limiting government power, but more recently it became associated with government efforts to ensure individual welfare and the use of international law to promote liberty and justice abroad. Liberalism is often contrasted with realism. ***Neo-liberalism*** adds to the traditional view an emphasis on institution building and the work of international organizations, nongovernmental organizations, multinational corporations, and other nonstate actors. *See also* Realism.

Local ownership—The notion that the affected country must drive its own development needs and priorities even if transitional authority is in the hands of outsiders. Also called ***host country ownership***.

Mandate—In international relations, the term usually refers to a UN peacekeeping mission authorized by the UN Security Council under the auspices of the UN Charter, especially chapter 6 or 7. The term can also refer to electoral politics when a winning party interprets its victory as an endorsement of its campaign platform. *See also* Chapters 6 and 7 *and* Peacekeeping.

Marginalized groups—Groups that have been relegated to the fringes of society based on such factors as their ethnicity, religion, age, disability, gender, or sexual orientation. These groups are typically denied rights, opportunities, and resources because they are seen to deviate from mainstream norms. *See also* Vulnerable groups.

Mass atrocities—Large-scale and deliberate attacks on civilians. The victims of mass atrocities are typically targeted because of their identification as members of a group. This term usually refers to three legally defined international crimes: crimes against humanity, genocide, and war crimes. It can be used to refer to crimes of genocidal scope and intent without requiring a formal legal finding of genocide. *See also* Crimes against humanity, Genocide, *and* War crimes.

Media peacebuilding—The use of broadcast, print, and social media to promote a peaceful resolution of conflict. ***Conflict-sensitive journalism*** goes further by encouraging journalists to be aware of the effects their language and reporting can have on the conflict. ***Peace journalism*** is more agenda driven and approaches activism in its focus on the search for nonviolent solutions to conflict. Strategies include citizen media (blogs, wikis, and the like), social marketing, and media regulation. *See also* Information and communication technologies.

Mediation—A mode of negotiation in which a mutually acceptable third party helps the parties to a conflict find a solution that they cannot find by themselves. It is a three-sided political process in which the mediator builds and then draws upon relationships with the other two parties to help them reach a settlement. Unlike judges or arbitrators, mediators have no authority to decide the dispute between the parties, although powerful mediators may bring to the table considerable capability to influence the outcome. Mediators are typically from outside the conflict. Sometimes mediators are impartial and neutral, in other cases they have a strategic interest that motivates them to promote a negotiated outcome. Mediators may focus on facilitating communication and negotiation but they also may offer solutions and use leverage, including positive and negative incentives, to persuade the parties to achieve an agreement. *See also* Negotiation.

Metrics—The measurable indicators of progress, typically to assist in implementing an agreement. The most useful metrics gauge impact or outcomes—such as fewer weapons-related deaths, reduced child mortality, increased literacy, and reduced gender disparity in education—rather than outputs. *See also* Indicators, Outcomes, *and* Outputs.

Monitoring—The close observation of an activity or process, usually by an independent party or party from another country. It can refer to elections, to military or political actions as part of confidence-building measures, or, in capacity building, to the ongoing evaluation of a project to assess the process and impact and to redirect the project if necessary. Many writers refer to ***monitoring and evaluation (M&E)*** as a single term, since they are so closely connected. *See also* Evaluation.

Moral hazard—The controversial idea that some groups are more likely to rebel and thereby provoke retaliation if they believe it will result in significant humanitarian intervention. The term has been borrowed from the financial and economic fields, where it refers to a party increasing its exposure to risk because it is insured.

Multicultural—*See* Culture.

Multilateral—Involving more than two nations or parties. The United Nations and the World Trade Organization are multilateral organizations. ***Multilateral negotiations*** are highly complex coalition-building efforts that may involve states, nonstate actors, and international organizations.

Multitrack diplomacy—*See* Tracks of diplomacy.

Mutually hurting stalemate—A situation in which neither party thinks it can win a given conflict without incurring excessive loss, and in which both are suffering from a continuation of fighting. A mutually hurting stalemate can be a precondition for ripeness, a propitious moment for third-party mediation. There is substantial literature concerning the conditions, implications, and utility of "ripeness" as an analytical tool. *See also* Ripeness.

Narrative versus story—In international relations, a narrative is much more than just a story. It might be understood as a people's most strongly held beliefs about the way history has unfolded, not only an explanation of events but also a separate view of reality. In divided societies—where there has been protracted conflict—narratives are often parallel. The differing groups do not agree on what occurred in the distant past and this core disagreement often causes them to dispute what has happened in recent times.

Nationalism—A strong sense of loyalty to a particular nation, often combined with the belief that nation should be an independent state. Elements of cohesion are provided by such factors as language, religion, historical experience, and physical closeness, although no one factor seems to be necessary. Such bonds subjectively define a group of people as different from their neighbors. *See also* State versus nation.

Nation versus state—*See* State versus nation.

Needs assessment—A type of assessment used to determine priorities and resource allocation. In some definitions it is synonymous with a baseline assessment and includes gathering data and analyzing it to determine which needs to focus on. In other definitions it also includes creating and implementing a plan of action and evaluating the results. *See also* Assessment.

Negative peace versus positive peace—Negative peace refers to the absence of violence. Positive peace refers to a society where there is no structural violence or social injustice. *See also* Peace.

Negotiation—The process of communication and bargaining between parties seeking to arrive at a mutually acceptable outcome on issues of shared concern. The process typically involves compromise and concessions and is designed to result in an agreement, although sometimes a party participates in negotiations for other reasons (to score propaganda points or to appease domestic political forces, for example). ***Prenegotiation*** refers to preliminary talks to agree on such issues as the format, procedures, time frame, who will participate, and sometimes the scope of the formal talks. ***Endgame*** refers to the final stages of a negotiation, when substantive progress has been made but important details remain to be resolved and the agreement hammered into final form. *See also* Mediation.

Neutrality—A deliberate policy of not taking sides in hostilities or not engaging in controversies involving politics, race, religion, or ideology. *See also* Impartiality.

Nongovernmental organization (NGO)—A private, self-governing, nonprofit organization dedicated to advancing objectives such as alleviating human suffering; promoting education, health care, economic development, environmental protection, human rights, and conflict resolution; and encouraging the strengthening of democratic institutions and civil society. Some people use the term ***international nongovernmental organization* (INGO)** to differentiate those organizations that transcend national boundaries from local NGOs. Also known as ***private voluntary organizations***, ***civic associations***, ***nonprofits***, and ***charitable organizations***. *See also* Civil society.

Nonprofit versus not-for-profit—Generally interchangeable terms, though nonprofit can indicate a formal legal existence or charter.

Nonstate actor—A large category that includes nongovernmental organizations, multinational corporations, media, terrorist groups, warlords, insurgents, criminal organizations, religious groups, trade unions, universities, and diaspora communities. Most types of nonstate actors would be considered part of civil society. Also called ***nonofficial actors***.

Nonviolent civic action—An action, usually undertaken by a group of people, to persuade someone else to change their behavior. Examples include strikes, boycotts, marches, and demonstrations. Nonviolent civic action can be categorized into three main classes: protest and persuasion, noncooperation, and intervention. It operates on the precept that all political relationships require varying degrees of cooperation or acquiescence, which can be withdrawn. Nonviolent civic action is also known as ***strategic nonviolence, nonviolent resistance***, ***direct action***, ***civic mobilization,*** and ***civil resistance***. Gandhi used the term ***Satyagraha***, roughly translated as "firmness in truth," to describe his concept of nonviolent action.

Norms—A standard of conduct that individuals, organizations, or governments are expected to follow. Norms can be enforced formally (for example, through sanctions or through actions of the International Criminal Court) or informally (for example, through behind-the-scenes diplomatic efforts).

Outcomes—Measurable changes on social, economic, or other indicators arising from the delivery of outputs. *See also* Assessment, Evaluation, Metrics, *and* Monitoring.

Outputs—Results of products or services delivered (often called deliverables). *See also* Assessment, Evaluation, Metrics, *and* Monitoring.

Pacifism—The rejection of war or violence as a means of resolving conflict. Some pacifists reject violence under all circumstances, even self-defense. Others make exceptions for certain circumstances such as the Holocaust. Some pacifists will take part in noncombat activities such as providing medical care. For some, pacifism includes nonviolent action to promote justice and human rights, but it is not a precondition.

Pariah state—A state whose conduct is considered unacceptable to the international community or a group of powerful states, generally because that conduct is perceived as not conforming to international norms. As a result, the state may risk isolation, sanctions, or invasion. The classic example is apartheid South Africa. There are no universal standards for declaring a state a pariah, and the term is sometimes used very differently by different states or groups of states. The term is often used synonymously with ***rogue state***.

Parties to the conflict—Disputants can be divided into first or primary parties, those who have decision-making power and must be involved in any negotiation, and secondary parties, those who have a less direct stake but can affect the outcome by supporting or repudiating actions of the first parties.

Peace—The word peace evokes complex and sometimes contradictory interpretations and reactions. For some, peace means the absence of conflict; for others it means the end of violence or the formal cessation of hostilities; for still others, the return to resolving conflict by political means. Some define peace as the attainment of justice and social stability; for others it is economic well-being and basic freedom. Peace is often unstable, as sources of conflict are seldom completely resolved or eliminated. Since conflict is inherent in the human condition, the striving for peace is particularly strong in times of violent conflict. That said, a willingness to accommodate perpetrators of violence without resolving the sources of conflict—sometimes called peace at any price—may lead to greater conflict later. *See also* Negative peace versus positive peace.

Peace agreement—A formal agreement between parties to a violent conflict to end hostilities or to significantly transform them. According to the United Nations, there are five basic types of peace agreements, although they sometimes overlap and they do not all occur in every agreement: cease-fire, prenegotiation, interim or preliminary, comprehensive or framework, and implementation. The terms ***peace agreement*** and ***peace treaty*** are often used synonymously. *See also* Peace process *and* Treaty.

Peacebuilding—Originally conceived in the context of postconflict recovery efforts to promote reconciliation and reconstruction, the term peacebuilding has more recently taken on a broader meaning. It may include providing humanitarian relief, protecting human rights, ensuring security, establishing nonviolent modes of resolving conflicts, fostering reconciliation, providing trauma-healing services, repatriating refugees and resettling internally displaced persons, supporting broad-based education, and aiding in economic reconstruction. As such, it also includes conflict prevention in the sense of preventing the recurrence of violence, as well as conflict management and postconflict recovery. In a larger sense, peacebuilding involves a transformation toward more manageable, peaceful relationships and governance structures—the long-term process of addressing root causes and effects, reconciling differences, normalizing relations, and building institutions that can manage conflict without resorting to violence.

Peace dividend—The benefit a country receives from cutting back military spending, especially after the end of a war. It comes when spending is redirected to social programs or tax reductions.

Peace education—According to UNICEF, peace education is "the process of promoting the knowledge, skills, attitudes and values needed to bring about behaviour change that will enable children, youth, and adults to prevent conflict and violence, both overt and structural; to resolve conflict peacefully; and to create the conditions conducive to peace, whether at an interpersonal, intergroup, national, or international level." *See also* Education *and* Peace (and conflict) studies.

Peace enforcement—A coercive action undertaken with the authorization of the UN Security Council to end armed hostilities, restore a cease-fire, or enforce a peace agreement. Includes diplomatic and military measures usually carried out by a third-party or multinational force. Consent of the affected parties is not required. *See also* Chapters 6 and 7.

Peacekeeping—Traditionally, action undertaken to preserve peace where fighting has been halted and to assist in implementing agreements achieved by the peacemakers. Typically authorized by the UN Security Council under chapter 6 or 7 of the UN Charter, these operations usually include lightly armed military personnel and have the consent of the parties. The scope of peacekeeping activities has gradually broadened since the end of the Cold War to include civilian and humanitarian activities such as food distribution, electoral assistance, refugee return and reintegration, civilian protection and prevention of gender-based violence, restoration of transportation and other basic services, and establishing safe havens. In recent years, peacekeepers have been placed in areas where fighting is continuing, and their role is more to position themselves between hostile parties, a situation in which there is often a mismatch between their mandate and their capability.

Peacemaking—Activities to halt an ongoing conflict and bring hostile parties to agreement, usually by such methods as those identified in chapter 6 of the UN Charter: "Negotiation, enquiry, mediation, conciliation, arbitration, judicial settlement, resort to regional agencies or agreements, or other peaceful means." It typically involves negotiating an agreement between contending parties, often with the help of a third-party mediator. *See also* Conflict management.

Peace operation—A generic term that can encompass peacemaking, peacekeeping, peace enforcement, and peacebuilding, the lines between which are not always clear.

Peace process—The series of steps or phases in a negotiation or mediation that are necessary in order to eventually reach a peace agreement and sometimes to implement one. These steps are not necessarily sequential or linear. They may include confidence-building measures, risk-reduction strategies, good offices, fact-finding or observer missions, conciliation and mediation efforts, and deployment of international forces.

Peace (and conflict) studies—An interdisciplinary field that focuses on conflict analysis, conflict management, and conflict transformation; nonviolent sanctions; peacebuilding, peacekeeping, and peace enforcement; social and economic justice; war's causes and conduct; and international and domestic security. ***Peace research*** is a constituent element, drawing on the work of academicians and nongovernmental organizations alike; it generally refers to university-level work, whereas ***peace education*** encompasses all levels of study.

Pedagogy—The art or science of teaching, including instructional methods. ***Andragogy*** refers to teaching adults and focuses on factors such as experiential learning activities, relevance to work or home lives, and problem-centered approaches.

Policymakers—The individuals who have the authority to set the policy framework of a business or organization. In business, they would usually be members of the board of directors. In US government, they might include the president and White House aides, agency officials, specially appointed task forces, interest groups, private research organizations, and legislators. Typically, most or all interact in a complicated process that sets policies.

Political violence—The organized or systematic use of force, the motive for which is primarily political—that is, aimed at influencing government policy—rather than criminal. It can include terrorism, rebellion, war, conquest, revolution, oppression, and tyranny.

Positions versus interests—Broadly speaking, positions are what parties say they want. Interests are what they need. Interests are frequently unstated and may be difficult to identify. Often parties' interests are compatible, and hence negotiable, even when their positions do not seem to be. Focusing on underlying interests can help parties identify which issues are of most concern to them and to find solutions that might not be evident from their stated positions. Some analysts distinguish between interests and ***needs***, arguing that needs such as identity and security are more fundamental than interests. Some analysts also distinguish between interests and ***values***, the ideas individuals have about what is good or worthwhile.

Postconflict recovery—The long-term rebuilding of a society in the aftermath of violent conflict. It includes political, socioeconomic, and physical aspects such as disarming and reintegrating combatants, resettling internally displaced persons, reforming governmental institutions, promoting trauma work and reconciliation, delivering justice, restarting the economy, and rebuilding damaged infrastructure. Related terms include ***war-to-peace transitions*** and ***postconflict reconstruction.*** Recovery has a broader connotation than reconstruction, which implies an emphasis on physical aspects.

Power—The ability to influence others to get a particular outcome. It may involve coercing them with threats, providing inducements, or co-opting them. ***Hard power*** refers to the use of military and economic means to influence the behavior of others through coercion or inducements. ***Soft power*** refers to the ability to attract or co-opt others through one's values, policies, and performance. ***Smart power*** encompasses both hard and soft power, emphasizing the need to employ whatever tools—diplomatic, economic, military, political, legal, scientific, and cultural—are appropriate for the situation.

Power sharing—A system of governance in which different segments of society are provided a share of power. Traditionally this has meant coalition governments, minimum representation in government institutions, and decision-making requiring a high threshold or consensus. Power-sharing arrangements often increase the legitimacy of governments, especially in diverse societies, but because of their emphasis on group rights and consensus some lead to deadlock.

Practitioner—A person who is qualified to practice a particular occupation or profession. Most frequently used in the medical field but also used in the peacebuilding field to connote someone with specific skills, usually gained from practical experience in conflict situations.

Preventive diplomacy—Any official diplomatic action taken to prevent disputes from arising between parties, to prevent existing disputes from escalating into conflicts, and to limit the spread and impact of the latter when they occur. *See also* Conflict prevention.

Prisoner of war—A combatant captured in war, especially a member of a country's armed forces taken by the enemy during combat.

Problem-solving workshop—An informal, confidential dialogue that brings adversaries together to reevaluate their attitudes and think creatively about joint solutions. These face-to-face meetings occur outside diplomatic negotiations but may feed into them. *See also* Tracks of diplomacy.

Proliferation—Traditionally, this term has referred to the spread of nuclear weapons and other weapons of mass destruction, including chemical and biological weapons. In conflict management, however, proliferation also refers to the illicit trade in small arms and light weapons (everything from pistols to machine guns to anti-tank missiles and landmines), the kinds of weapons that fuel most violent conflicts. The term can also refer to all conventional weapons (meaning all weapons short of weapons of mass destruction).

Protection of civilians (POC)—Definitions of this term vary considerably, usually depending on the associated institutional mandate. The UN Security Council first identified POC as a duty in its own right in 1998. The UN website currently defines POC as "all necessary action, up to and including the use of force, aimed at preventing or responding to threats of physical violence against civilians, within capabilities and areas of operations, and without prejudice to the responsibility of the host government to protect its civilians." Not all UN peacekeeping missions have a protection mandate, although most current ones do. The African Union has developed its own guidelines on POC in peace support operations. In addition, numerous external actors undertake protection activities, including UN agencies, the ICRC, IGOs, NGOs, corporations, security companies, and the media. *See also* Responsibility to protect.

Proximity talks—Diplomatic discussions conducted through an intermediary, usually because the disputants are nearby but unwilling to meet face-to-face. The hope is that proximity talks will lead to direct negotiations. A closely related term is ***shuttle diplomacy***, which usually means that the intermediary travels back and forth between the disputants' places of business.

Public diplomacy—Advocacy openly directed at foreign publics in support of negotiations or broad policy positions and to enlist their backing for a particular position or outcome.

Quartet—In peacebuilding, Quartet refers to four groups or organizations that work together to bring about peace in a specific conflict. For the Israeli-Palestinian peace process, it refers to the United Nations, United States, European Union, and Russia. For Tunisia, it refers to four civil society groups that brokered a compromise among the country's political factions, resulting in the selection of a new prime minister and ratification of a new constitution and presidential elections later in 2014. The Tunisian groups were awarded the Nobel Peace Prize in 2015 for their efforts.

Radicalization—The process by which an individual or group adopts extreme political, social, or religious beliefs. It is a controversial term because it is often considered a necessary precursor to terrorism, although many scholars disagree with that interpretation. Most scholars seem to agree that multiple pathways can lead to radicalization. ***De-radicalization*** is the process of cognitive disassociation from a violent group identity and ideology, and at times phyisical separation. *See also* Countering violent extremism, Extremism, *and* Violent extremism.

Rapprochement—The restoration or establishment of improved relations between previously estranged states and governments.

Rational choice theory—From the field of economics, the theory that people act rationally, that is, they try to maximize gains and minimize losses. Consequently, it should be possible to build models to make predictions about future actions.

Readiness—In mediation, this term means having operational and political capacity (requisite people and skills, necessary resources and institutional support, a solid and durable mandate, and the right leadership) and strategic and diplomatic capacity (the ability to catalyze international coalitions and orchestrate initiatives).

Realism or realpolitik—A school of thought that views the international system as inherently chaotic and sees the state as the primary actor in international politics; the state's goal is therefore the pursuit of power to protect its interests and ensure its survival. ***Neorealism***, or ***structural realism***, adds an emphasis on how the structural constraints of the international system (such as alliances, international agreements, accepted norms, globalization, dependency) affect the behavior of individual states. *See also* Liberalism.

Reconciliation—The long-term process by which parties to a dispute build trust, learn to live cooperatively, and create a stable peace. It can happen at the individual, community, and national level. It may involve dialogue, admissions of guilt, apology, judicial processes, truth commissions, ritual forgiveness, and *sulha* (a traditional Arabic form of ritual forgiveness and restitution).

Reconstruction—The process of rebuilding degraded, damaged, or destroyed political, socioeconomic, and physical infrastructure of a country or territory to create a foundation for long-term development. *See also* Postconflict recovery.

Red Crescent—*See* Red Cross and Red Crescent.

Red Cross and Red Crescent—The International Red Cross and Red Crescent Movement is an international humanitarian movement consisting of three distinct organizations that are legally independent of each other but share basic principles, objectives, and symbols. The International Committee of the Red Cross (ICRC) was founded in 1863 in Geneva and has a unique authority under international humanitarian law to protect the life and dignity of victims of armed conflicts. It draws its legal status from the Geneva Conventions so it is not technically an NGO, but its basic principles are accepted by the NGO community. The International Federation of Red Cross and Red Crescent Societies (IFRC) was founded in 1919 and coordinates activities among the 190 National Red Cross and Red Crescent Societies. (Red Crescent societies are the Red Cross's counterparts in Islamic countries.) Also based in Geneva, the IFRC leads and organizes, in cooperation with the national societies, relief assistance to large-scale emergencies. National Red Cross and Red Crescent Societies work in their home countries, often taking on additional humanitarian tasks not specifically defined by law or mandate.

Refoulement—The forcible return of refugees or asylum seekers to a country where they might be persecuted. ***Nonrefoulement*** is a principle of international law that considers it illegal to do so. *See also* Repatriation.

Reframing—Looking at a problem from new perspectives in order to find ways to reduce tensions or break a deadlock. It is the process of redefining a situation—seeing a conflict in a new way, usually based on input from other people.

Refugee—A person forced to leave their home, in particular as a result of armed conflict, generalized violence, violations of human rights, or natural or human-made disasters, and has crossed an internationally recognized state border. Some sources restrict use of the term refugee to individuals with a well-founded fear of being persecuted for reasons of race, religion, nationality, membership of a social group, or political opinion. *See also* Internally displaced person.

Regime type—The set of political institutions by which a government of a state is organized. They include democracy, dictatorship, monarchy, and theocracy. Many governments include in their official name a specific type, such as commonwealth, emirate, federation, kingdom, or republic.

Regional organization—The intergovernmental entities that focus on a specific geographic area or group of countries, such as the African Union, Arab League, Association of Southeast Asian Nations, European Union, and Organization of American States.

Reintegration—The reestablishment of social, familial, and community ties and positive participation in society. In international relations, it may refer to soldiers in a military or paramilitary unit, or fighters returning from a foreign conflict such as the ones in Afghanistan or Syria. *See also* Disarmament, demobilization, and reintegration.

Religion—A human response to a perceived non-physical reality concerning the origin, meaning, and purpose of life. Typically organized by communities into a shared system of symbols, rituals, institutions, and practices. Religions are internally complex and dynamic, manifesting differently across time and place. For example, Islam in Indonesia and in Iran may be practiced and expressed differently. They also contain a range of positions on any one issue. For example, Buddhism contains ideas that both promote and challenge gender equality.

Rent seeking—A somewhat confusing term that does not refer to rent in the usual sense but instead refers to lobbying the government for special privileges such as a subsidy, a tariff on competing goods, or a regulation that hampers competition.

Reparations—The compensation for war damage by a defeated state, or compensation to victims of mass crime committed by a former regime.

Repatriation—The return of a person, usually a prisoner of war or refugee, to their own country or legal home. It can be voluntary or involuntary, with or without incentives. *See also* Refoulement.

Resilience—The ability to bounce back, to successfully adapt to adversity, trauma, tragedy, threats, or other significant sources of stress. More specifically, USAID defines it as "the ability of people, households, communities, countries, and systems to mitigate, adapt to, and recover from shocks and stresses in a manner that reduces chronic vulnerability and facilitates inclusive growth." Traditionally, the development community tended to focus on natural and human-made disasters but more recently they have included economic events such as recessions. An increasing emphasis on measuring impact has resulted in the use of multiple indicators to assess such factors as reduced need for assistance, depth of poverty, and malnutrition levels. The concept of resilience has been increasingly employed in the conflict management field. *See also* Fragility *and* Vulnerable groups.

Resource curse or the paradox of plenty—The argument that mismanagement of natural resource abundance often produces weak states, little to no economic growth, and conflict. In the ***Dutch disease***, abundant natural resources contribute to economic stagnation because capital and labor only focus on the booming natural resources for tradeable exports. In the ***honeypot effect***, abundant supplies of valuable local resources create incentives for rebel groups to form and fight to capture the resource. In ***rentier states***, governments that take in a significant amount of revenue (rents or excess profits) from natural resource exports are prone to corruption because they can afford to buy off or intimidate opponents.

Responsibility to protect (R2P)—A recently developed concept, R2P asserts that states have an ethical and legal responsibility to protect their people against genocide, war crimes, crimes against humanity, and ethnic cleansing, but if a state is unable or unwilling to do so, that responsibility falls to the international community, which may intervene militarily in extreme cases. A controversial concept, R2P was endorsed by all members of the United Nations at the 2005 World Summit, but some states have since expressed doubts. R2P includes the responsibility to prevent, react, and rebuild, and therefore can be applied to all parts of the conflict curve, for those who accept its far-reaching implications. The term is sometimes abbreviated as RTP. *See also* Protection of civilians.

Restorative justice—An approach to justice that emphasizes a cooperative process involving victims, offenders, and the community. It focuses on repairing the harm done by criminal behavior, in contrast to retributive justice, which emphasizes punishing offenders. *See also* Justice.

Right of return—The right of any person to reenter his or her country of origin. The Universal Declaration of Human Rights states that "everyone has the right to leave any country, including his own, and to return to his country." Many countries have enacted laws concerning the right of return, mostly to facilitate the immigration of members of diaspora communities.

Ripeness—A period in a conflict where parties are most likely to be open to mediation, usually due to conditions of a mutually hurting stalemate. A conflict is said to be ripe when it has reached such a stalemate and all the parties have determined that their alternatives to negotiation will not get them what they want or need. It is also possible for third parties to help create a perception of ripeness by introducing alternative ways of framing a conflict or by providing actual incentives or disincentives. *See also* Mutually hurting stalemate.

Risk management—The identification of risks to an organization and the development of strategies and techniques to confront them. Such risks might include accidents, natural disasters, wars, and financial issues.

Rule of law—A principle of governance in which all persons and institutions, public and private, including the state itself, are accountable to laws that are publicly announced, equally enforced and independently adjudicated, and consistent with international human rights norms and standards. The drafting of laws must be transparent, and they must be applied fairly and without arbitrariness. In addition, all persons must have access to justice—the ability to seek and obtain a remedy through informal or formal institutions of justice.

Rules of engagement (ROE)—The rules delineating the circumstances and limitations under which force should be used by the military or police, including when, where, and against whom.

Sanctions—Actions typically taken by countries to influence the behavior of other parties. Sanctions can be diplomatic (reduction of diplomatic ties, for example), economic (embargoes, freezing of assets), personal (travel bans), or cultural (limits on educational exchanges). The effectiveness of sanctions has been much debated, as have the detrimental effects on innocent civilians. In an effort to avoid those negative effects, some analysts have advocated using ***smart sanctions***, meaning targeted actions such as arms embargoes, asset freezes, and travel bans that focus on key individuals and organizations and are intended to reduce damage to the general population. *See also* Incentives and disincentives.

Security—Traditionally, security has meant freedom from military attack and has been synonymous with ***national security***. In addition, a state can enter into alliances that provide ***collective security***. More recently, the concept has expanded to include environmental and economic concerns. The term ***human security*** has been used to emphasize the need to focus on the needs of the individual, including freedom from fear and freedom from want, as well as specific needs such as food security. *See also* Human security.

Security dilemma—The theory that actions by a state to increase its security, especially by military enhancements, will cause other states to react similarly, resulting in a spiral that will increase the likelihood of conflict, even if neither side wants it. Critics argue that collective security arrangements can greatly mitigate the most dangerous effects of this spiral.

Security sector—Those who are, or should be, responsible for protecting the state and communities within the state. Includes military, paramilitary, intelligence, border control, and police services as well as civilian structures responsible for oversight and control of the security forces and for the administration of justice.

Security sector reform (SSR)—The policies, plans, programs, and activities that a government undertakes to improve the way it provides safety, security, and justice.

Self-determination—The right of a people to determine their own political status. That could mean full independence, or it could mean a greater degree of autonomy and linguistic or religious identity within an existing state. *See also* Autonomy.

Sexual violence—A form of gender-based violence, sexual violence refers to any act, attempt, or threat of a sexual nature that results in, or is likely to result in, physical or psychological harm. It includes all forms of sexual exploitation and abuse, such as rape, spousal battering, sexual abuse of children, dowry-related violence, marital rape, female genital mutilation, sexual harassment and intimidation at work and in educational institutions, and trafficking and forced prostitution. Sexual violence has also been used as a tool of ethnic cleansing, as documented in Bosnia and Darfur, for example. *See also* Gender-based violence *and* Gender sensitivity.

Shuttle diplomacy—*See* Proximity talks.

Side payment—A payment or other reward made to a party or parties to induce them to join an agreement. Such inducements frequently take the form of aid or trade preferences.

Simulation—An educational exercise that helps individuals learn about conflict situations and how to deal with them. It may include role-playing and other experiential activities. Often conducted in person but increasingly online. *See also* Tabletop exercise.

Social capital—*See* Human capital.

Social cohesion—The willingness of members of a society to cooperate in order to promote the well-being of all members, fight exclusion, and increase upward mobility.

Social contract—An implicit agreement among individuals or between them and their government in which they give up part of their freedom in exchange for such benefits as social order and security.

Social media—Internet-based applications that allow users with little technical knowledge to easily create and share content. They include blogs; wikis; social networking websites such as Facebook, Twitter, and LinkedIn; photo- and video-sharing sites such as Instagram and YouTube; news aggregation sites; and social bookmarking sites. *See also* Media peacebuilding.

Social well-being—A situation in which basic human needs are met and people are able to coexist peacefully in communities with opportunities for advancement. It is characterized by access to basic services (water, food, shelter, and health services), provision of primary and secondary education, return or resettlement of displaced persons, and restoration of social fabric and community life. Social well-being is considered critical for societies emerging from conflict—equally as important as security, rule of law, economic development, and good governance.

Soft power—*See* Power.

Sovereignty—The principle that states have primacy over their internal affairs. It is the basis for the international norm of noninterference in the affairs of independent and self-governing states. In practice, however, state sovereignty is not absolute and states restrict or share authority either through their own volition (for example, through treaties or consent to peacekeeping) or through the exercise of UN Security Council authority. *See also* Autonomy *and* Responsibility to protect.

Spoiler—A person or group that seeks to block or sabotage a peace process or the implementation of an agreement, usually because it threatens their power and interests. *See also* Conflict entrepreneur.

Stability operations—An evolving and much-disputed term, stability operations is now generally used to describe US military activities undertaken to maintain or reestablish a safe and secure environment and provide essential governmental services, emergency infrastructure reconstruction, and humanitarian relief—primarily in support of other US agencies, such as the Department of State and USAID, or an international organization.

State versus nation—A state, or country, is a sovereign, self-governing political entity, for example any state in the United Nations. (The term "state" is also used to refer to a division of a federal system, as in the United States.) A nation is a group of people who feel bound by a common language, culture, religion, history, or ethnicity, such as the Kurds, who reside mostly in Iran, Iraq, Syria, and Turkey, and the Basque, who inhabit parts of northern Spain and southern France. A ***nation-state*** occurs when a nation and a state largely coincide, for example Egypt, Hungary, and Japan. The terms ***state building*** and ***nation building*** are most often used as synonyms to refer to the process of building or rebuilding state institutions to create a legitimate and sustainable state.

Strategy versus tactics—Strategy is the overarching, long-term process or plan to attain desired objectives as efficiently as possible, usually in competition with others who are developing similar activities. Tactics are limited and particular actions decided on short-term bases. If conducted efficiently, the choice of tactics will be informed by a strategy. For example, the strategy might call for a boycott, but the tactics might include picketing.

Summit meeting—A gathering of heads of government. At most summit meetings, the principals' main role is to put the finishing touches on agreements that have already been negotiated at a lower level. Summits are also useful in giving leaders opportunities to judge firsthand each other's character and mode of operating.

Supranational—An authority that is above the state, usually in prescribed areas. The clearest example is the European Union, which has a common political structure and can make certain decisions by majority vote. Somewhat more ambiguously, the UN Security Council can exercise executive policy in relation to peace and security matters (articles 24 and 25 of the UN Charter).
It is a controversial term because it is seen by some to impinge unduly upon state sovereignty.

Sustainability—The ability to maintain something indefinitely. In capacity building, it means creating capacity that will remain in place and effective even after the initiative ends or the intervener departs. In development, it means meeting the needs of the present without compromising the ability of future generations to meet their own needs. In the context of natural resources, sustainability refers to harnessing natural resources without depleting them. In the broader context of the environment, it means satisfying basic human needs while maintaining environmental quality.

Tabletop exercise (TTX)—An activity in which key personnel discuss simulated scenarios in an informal setting, usually with an experienced facilitator. Commonly used by the military and emergency agencies to test plans and procedures. *See also* Simulation.

Terrorism—The use of violence, typically against civilians, for the purpose of attracting attention to a political cause, encouraging others to join in, or intimidating opponents into concessions. Some terrorists aim to provoke a harsh reaction by their opponents that will in turn generate support for the terrorists' issues. Although the distinctions are not always clear, ***state terrorism*** generally refers to acts committed by governments either domestically or abroad, while ***state-sponsored terrorism*** refers to support for nonstate actors that commit terrorist acts.

Theory of change—In peacebuilding, how a particular intervention will bring about change. It requires identifying the desired outcomes and deciding on the interventions that will achieve those outcomes. Most people operate under a theory of change, even though they may not acknowledge it. The theory is not static but can be refined as evidence accumulates.

Third party—An individual or group that helps disputants resolve their problem, typically as mediators, arbitrators, or conciliators. They can be insiders or outsiders, impartial or partial. Neutrality is required in some cases, but the ability to put pressure on one or both sides through carrots or sticks can be useful.

Time, attitudes toward—Time management in a postconflict environment is often affected by attitudes or values not always shared by interveners, such as a need to cultivate personal relationships before completing a task, a strong belief in fate or the inability to control one's destiny, or a general focus on the past instead of the future. Temporal orientation can also be understood in terms of the difference between ***monochronicity*** and ***polychronicity***—preferring to do one thing at a time versus engaging in several things simultaneously, which often involves a blurring of personal and professional space.

Tracks of diplomacy—Over the years, scholars have delineated several levels of diplomacy. Tracks 1 and 2 are the most frequently used terms. A composite term is multitrack diplomacy.

Track 1 diplomacy—Official discussions typically involving high-level political and military leaders and focusing on cease-fires, peace talks, and treaties and other agreements.

Track 2 diplomacy—Unofficial dialogue and problem-solving activities aimed at building relationships and encouraging new thinking that can inform the official process. Track 2 activities such as facilitated workshops typically involve influential academic, religious, and NGO leaders and other civil society actors who can interact more freely than high-ranking officials. ***Track 1.5*** is sometimes used to indicate a situation in which official and nonofficial actors work together to resolve conflicts.

Track 3 diplomacy—People-to-people diplomacy undertaken by individuals and private groups to encourage interaction and understanding between hostile communities and increase awareness and empowerment. Normally focused at the grassroots level, it often involves organizing meetings and conferences, generating media exposure, and political and legal advocacy for marginalized people and communities.

Tracks of diplomacy (cont.)

Multitrack diplomacy—Efforts that operate on several tracks simultaneously, including official and unofficial conflict resolution efforts, citizen and scientific exchanges, international business negotiations, international cultural and athletic activities, and other cooperative efforts. These efforts could be led by governments, professional organizations, businesses, churches, media, private citizens, training and educational institutes, activists, and funders.

Training—The development of particular skills or knowledge, with the goal of improving someone's capacity and performance, and also updating those skills. The latter is often referred to as professional development. *See also* Human capital.

Transitional justice—A process that addresses large-scale human rights abuses in an effort to establish the truth of what happened and why, acknowledge the suffering of victims, hold perpetrators accountable, compensate for wrongs, prevent future abuses, and promote social healing. War crimes tribunals are perhaps the best-known example. Some mechanisms are judicial, such as tribunals. Others are not, such as trauma-healing programs, reconciliation projects, reparations, and monuments or war memorials.

Translation versus interpreting—Translation refers to the production of a written text in another language, while interpreting refers to oral or sign-language communication. Both require skilled professionals because cultural differences are reflected in language and seemingly equivalent words can carry different meanings.

Transnational actors—Actors whose actions cross borders. They include intergovernmental organizations, multinational corporations, international nongovernmental organizations, and many religious organizations, as well as international terrorist networks and criminal networks.

Transparency—The visibility or accessibility of information regarding decision-making and financial practices, such that stakeholders have not only access to the decision-making process but also the ability to influence it.

Treaty—A formal and mutually binding written agreement between two or more states or other political authorities. Usually ratified by the state's legislative authority. ***Accord*** also refers to a formal agreement, but sometimes implies a status below that of a treaty. ***Convention*** typically addresses major interstate issues, for example the Geneva Conventions on the rules of warfare or the Convention on Biological Diversity. Some conventions have enforcement mechanisms, others do not. ***Protocol*** sometimes refers to an original draft of a document, the record of an agreement, or an amendment to an agreement.

Tribunal—In international law, this term is sometimes used for courts set up for special purposes, such as the International Criminal Tribunal for Rwanda or the International Criminal Tribunal for the former Yugoslavia, which were established by the UN Security Council.

Trigger—An event that initiates or accelerates a conflict, such as the assassination of a leader, election fraud, or a political scandal.

Truth (and reconciliation) commission or truth and justice commission—An official body, usually set up by states after periods of state-perpetrated violence, whose main task is to establish a record of wrongdoing as part of an overall process of catharsis and reconciliation. In rare cases, they are empowered to grant full or partial amnesty in exchange for full disclosure. Some commissions also address issues of reparation and rehabilitation. *See also* Reconciliation.

Violence—Physical or psychological force that injures, abuses, damages, or destroys people or property. In international relations, violent conflict typically refers to a clash of political interests between organized groups characterized by a sustained and large-scale use of force. Norwegian sociologist Johan Galtung identified three types of violence. ***Personal*** *or* ***direct violence*** involves killing, maiming, bullying, sexual assault, or emotional manipulation. ***Structural*** *or* ***indirect violence*** refers to inequalities built into the social system, such as institutionalized racism and sexism or inequalities in income distribution. ***Cultural*** *or* ***symbolic violence*** entails those aspects of culture that justify or legitimize direct or structural violence. Cultural violence also comprises underlying attitudes and unexamined assumptions about others or the way the world ought to work. *See also* Conflict *and* War.

Violent extremism—A broad term, much disputed. It is often defined as supporting or using violence to achieve ideological, religious, social, economic, or political goals. For most people, the term is broadly synonymous with terrorism. Presumably, the term would not apply to the legitimate use of force by a state; however, the definition of legitimate is disputed. *See also* Countering violent extremism, Extremism, *and* Radicalization.

Vulnerable groups—Traditionally, groups that have difficulty coping with and recovering from natural hazards and disasters, acts of oppression, and social exclusion. More recently, the term has been applied to social vulnerabilities such as human rights abuses, poverty, and malnutrition. It includes such groups as children, pregnant women, elderly people, malnourished people, and people who are ill or immuno-compromised.

War—Sustained fighting between conventional military forces, paramilitary forces, or guerrillas. Famously described by Carl von Clausewitz in the nineteenth century as "continuation of politics by other means." It can vary from low-intensity but continuing conflict or civil anarchy to all-out "hot" war. Some sources say that an armed conflict must cause one thousand or more reported battle deaths in a calendar year to be considered a war. ***Conventional war*** uses the arsenal of official armed forces (small arms, artillery, missile launchers) but excludes weapons of mass destruction. ***Limited war*** is war for objectives declared by those conducting it to be narrow and limited. ***Total war*** means unrestricted warfare, in which the laws of war are disregarded. *See also* Civil war, Guerrilla war, *and* Just war theory.

War crimes—Any offenses committed during armed conflict in violation of the laws of war or international humanitarian law, described fully in the Rome Statute of the International Criminal Court, article 8. Most war crimes are perpetrated against noncombatant and civilian populations; they include murder, torture, deportation, rape, the taking of hostages, and forced labor.

Watchlist—A list of countries at risk for specific concerns, maintained by government agencies or nongovernmental organizations as an early-warning mechanism. There are watchlists for crimes against humanity, for terrorism, for famines, and for humanitarian emergencies, among others. Some watchlists focus on individuals or groups suspected of planning crimes, other lists focus on countries that might be at risk.

Weapons of mass destruction (WMD)—Typically refers to nuclear, biological, or chemical weapons. Weapons not in this category are generally called conventional weapons, regardless of their destructive power.

Whole-of-government approach—The collaborative efforts of a government's departments and agencies to achieve a shared goal. Also known as ***interagency approach***. ***Unity of effort*** and ***unity of purpose*** are sometimes used to describe cooperation among all actors, government and otherwise.

Window of opportunity—A short period during which the chances of success in an endeavor are greatly increased. In negotiations, it is often produced by a change of leadership, an altered military situation, or an external event that affects the conflict. After the devastating 2004 tsunami, for example, the Aceh rebels were more willing to negotiate with the Indonesian government.

Win-win versus zero-sum—In a ***win-win*** or ***positive-sum*** outcome, everyone wins, usually through cooperation and joint problem solving. In a ***win-lose*** or ***zero-sum*** outcome, one side wins only if the other side loses; zero-sum thinking typically motivates parties to take an adversarial approach. In a ***lose-lose*** or ***negative-sum*** outcome, all parties lose. These terms originated in ***game theory***, which comes from the field of mathematics and analyzes behavior in specific situations. *See also* Game theory.

World Bank—According to the World Bank website, the term World Bank refers only to the International Bank for Reconstruction and Development (IBRD) and the International Development Association (IDA). The IBRD aims to reduce poverty in middle-income and creditworthy poorer countries, while the IDA focuses on the world's poorest countries. The term World Bank Group incorporates those two institutions plus three closely associated entities: the International Finance Corporation (IFC), the Multilateral Investment Guarantee Agency (MIGA), and the International Centre for the Settlement of Investment Disputes (ICSID).

ZOPA (zone of possible agreement)—*See* Bargaining.

ABBREVIATIONS

The following list contains abbreviations and acronyms for some of the organizations, concepts, and terms frequently encountered in the work of peacebuilding.

ADR	alternative dispute resolution
ASEAN	Association of Southeast Asian Nations
AU	African Union
BATNA	best alternative to a negotiated agreement
CBM	confidence-building measure
CIMIC	civil-military cooperation
CIS	Commonwealth of Independent States
CSO	civil society organization
CVE	countering violent extremism
DCAF	(Geneva Centre for the) Democratic Control of Armed Forces
DDR	disarmament, demobilization, and reintegration
DOD	Department of Defense, US
DOJ	Department of Justice, US
DOS	Department of State, US
DPA	Department of Political Affairs, UN
DPKO	Department of Peacekeeping Operations, UN
E&T	education and training
ECCAS	Economic Community of Central African States

ECOWAS	Economic Community of West African States
EU	European Union
FAO	Food and Agriculture Organization
GBV	gender-based violence
IASC	Inter-Agency Standing Committee, UN and others (coordination of humanitarian assistance)
IBRD	International Bank for Reconstruction and Development (World Bank Group)
IC	international community
ICAF	Interagency Conflict Assessment Framework, US
ICC	International Criminal Court
ICJ	International Court of Justice
ICRC	International Committee of the Red Cross
ICTs	information and communication technologies
IDA	Institute for Defense Analyses
IDA	International Development Association (World Bank Group)
IDP	internally displaced person
IFAD	International Fund for Agricultural Development
IFC	International Finance Corporation
IFI	international financial institution
IFRC	International Federation of Red Cross and Red Crescent Societies
IGO	intergovernmental organization
IHL	international humanitarian law
ILO	International Labour Organization
IMF	International Monetary Fund
INGO	international nongovernmental organization
IO	international organization
IOM	International Organization for Migration
LAS	League of Arab States (formal name of Arab League)
M&E	monitoring and evaluation
MCC	Millennium Challenge Corporation, US
MDG	Millennium Development Goal, UN

MOU	memorandum of understanding
NATO	North Atlantic Treaty Organization
NGO	nongovernmental organization
NVC	nonviolent civic action
OAS	Organization of American States
OCHA	Office for the Coordination of Humanitarian Affairs, UN
OECD	Organization for Economic Co-operation and Development
OHCHR	Office of the High Commissioner for Human Rights, UN
OIC	Organization of the Islamic Conference
OSCE	Organization for Security and Co-operation in Europe
POC	protection of civilians
R2P	responsibility to protect (sometimes RTP)
ROE	rules of engagement
SDG	Sustainable Development Goal, UN
SRSG	Special Representative of the Secretary General
SSR	security sector reform
TTX	tabletop exercise
UNDP	United Nations Development Programme
UNESCO	United Nations Educational, Scientific, and Cultural Organization
UNGA	United Nations General Assembly
UN-Habitat	United Nations Human Settlements Programme
UNHCR	(Office of the) United Nations High Commissioner for Refugees
UNICEF	United Nations Children's Fund
UNODC	United Nations Office on Drugs and Crime
UNSC	United Nations Security Council
UNTFHS	United Nations Trust Fund for Human Security
USAID	United States Agency for International Development
USIP	United States Institute of Peace

WFP	World Food Programme
WHO	World Health Organization
WMD	weapons of mass destruction
ZOPA	zone of possible agreement

SOURCES CONSULTED

Berghof Foundation. "Berghof Glossary on Conflict Transformation." Berlin: Berghof Foundation for Conflict Studies, 2012. www.berghof-foundation.org/publications /glossary.

Bolling, Rojan. "List of Frameworks for Conflict Analysis." *The Broker*, January 21, 2015. www.thebrokeronline.eu/Articles/List-of-Frameworks-for-Conflict-Analysis.

Boutros-Ghali, Boutros. *An Agenda for Peace: Preventive Diplomacy, Peacemaking, and Peacekeeping*. New York: United Nations, 1992.

Burgess, Guy, and Heidi Burgess, eds. "Glossary." Beyond Intractability Project. Boulder: University of Colorado, Conflict Information Consortium. www.beyond intractability.org/library/glossary.

Cohen, Raymond. *Negotiating Across Cultures: International Communication in an Interdependent World*, 2nd ed. Washington, DC: US Institute of Peace Press, 1997.

Crocker, Chester A., Fen Osler Hampson, and Pamela Aall, eds. *Herding Cats: Multiparty Mediation in a Complex World*. Washington, DC: US Institute of Peace Press, 1999.

———. *Managing Conflict in a World Adrift*. Washington, DC: US Institute of Peace Press, 2015.

Evans, Graham, and Jeffrey Newnham. *The Penguin Dictionary of International Relations*. London: Penguin, 1998.

Fisher, Roger, William Ury, and Bruce Patton. *Getting to Yes: Negotiating Agreement Without Giving In*, 2nd ed. New York: Penguin, 1991.

Freeman, Chas. W., Jr. *The Diplomat's Dictionary*, 2nd ed. Washington, DC: US Institute of Peace Press, 2010.

Human Security Report Project. *Mini-Atlas of Human Security*. Washington, DC: World Bank Publications, 2008. www.hsrgroup.org/our-work/publications /miniatlas.aspx.

Kurtz, Lester R., editor in chief. *Encyclopedia of Violence, Peace, and Conflict*, 2nd ed., 3 vols. Oxford: Academic Press/Elsevier, 2008.

Lederach, John Paul. *Building Peace: Sustainable Reconciliation in Divided Societies*. Washington, DC: US Institute of Peace Press, 1997.

Lund, Michael S. *Preventing Violent Conflicts: A Strategy for Preventive Diplomacy*. Washington, DC: US Institute of Peace Press, 1996.

Miller, Christopher E., and Mary E. King. *Glossary of Terms and Concepts in Peace and Conflict Studies*, 2nd ed. Addis Ababa: University for Peace Africa Programme, 2005. https://pdfs.semanticscholar.org/a3a2/d46ba0d752f49fba 8ddff1b72f7ba07fb16c.pdf.

Program on Negotiation. "Glossary." Cambridge, MA: Harvard Law School. www.pon.harvard.edu/glossary/.

Relief Web. "Glossary of Humanitarian Terms." New York: UN Office for the Coordination of Humanitarian Affairs, 2008. http://reliefweb.int/report/world /reliefweb-glossary-humanitarian-terms.

Schmid, Alex P. "Thesaurus and Glossary of Early Warning and Conflict Prevention Terms," abridged version. London: Forum on Early Warning and Early Response, 1998. http://reliefweb.int/sites/reliefweb.int/files/resources /82548F38DF3D1E73C1256C4D00368CA9-fewer-glossary-may98.pdf.

Search for Common Ground. "Commonly Used Terms." Washington, DC: SFCG, 2014. www.sfcg.org/wp-content/uploads/2014/02/commonly-used-terms.pdf.

Smith, Amy L., and David R. Smock. *Managing a Mediation Process*. Washington, DC: US Institute of Peace Press, 2008.

UK Department for International Development. "Glossary." London, August 2013.

www.gov.uk/government/publications/glossary-of-terms-used-by-the-department-for-international-development/glossary-of-terms-used-by-the-department-for-international-development.

United Nations. "Selected Glossary of Acronyms and Terms." In *Peacekeeping Operations: Principles and Guidelines*. New York: United Nations, 2008.

United States Government. *Compendium of Interagency and Associated Terms*. Washington, DC, July 2017. www.dtic.mil/doctrine/dod_dictionary/repository/interagency_associated_terms.pdf.

US Agency for International Development. *A Glossary on Violent Conflict*, 4th ed. Washington, DC: USAID, 2001. http://reliefweb.int/sites/reliefweb.int/files/resources/6C8E6652532FE542C12575DD00444F2D-USAID_may01.pdf.

US Institute of Peace. "Confronting Crimes Against Humanity." Study Guide Series on Peace and Conflict. Washington, DC: US Institute of Peace, 2008.

——. "Natural Resources, Conflict, and Conflict Resolution." Study Guide Series on Peace and Conflict. Washington, DC: US Institute of Peace, 2007.

US Institute of Peace and US Army Peacekeeping and Stability Operations Institute. *Guiding Principles for Stabilization and Reconstruction*. Washington, DC: US Institute of Peace Press, 2009.

World Bank. *World Development Report: Conflict, Security and Development*. Washington, DC: World Bank Group, 2011.

——. *World Development Report: Governance and the Law*. Washington, DC: World Bank Group, 2017.

Young, Nigel, editor in chief. *The Oxford International Encyclopedia of Peace*. New York: Oxford University Press, 2010.

Zartman, I. William. *Peacemaking in International Conflict: Methods and Techniques*, rev. ed. Washington, DC: US Institute of Peace Press, 2007.

INDEX

Page numbers in **bold** indicate main glossary terms.

UNITED STATES INSTITUTE OF PEACE PRESS

Since its inception in 1991, the United States Institute of Peace Press has published hundreds of influential books, reports, and briefs on the prevention, management, and peaceful resolution of international conflicts. All our books and reports arise from research and fieldwork sponsored by the Institute's many programs, and the Press is committed to extending the reach of the Institute's work by continuing to publish significant and sustainable publications for practitioners, scholars, diplomats, and students. In keeping with the best traditions of scholarly publishing, each work undergoes thorough peer review by external subject experts to ensure that the research and conclusions are balanced, relevant, and sound.

ABOUT THE EDITOR

Dan Snodderly is an editor and publishing consultant in Washington, DC. He served as USIP's director of publications from 1993 to 2004 and previously worked as an editor and writer at Cornell University Press and Encyclopaedia Britannica. The author of numerous articles and two books, he holds an AB degree in history from Harvard College.

ABOUT THE INSTITUTE

The United States Institute of Peace is an independent, nonpartisan institution established and funded by Congress. Its goals are to help prevent and resolve violent conflicts, promote postconflict peacebuilding, and increase conflict-management tools, capacity, and intellectual capital worldwide. The Institute does this by empowering others with knowledge, skills, and resources, as well as by its direct involvement in conflict zones around the globe.

BOARD OF DIRECTORS

PEACE TERMS

This book is set 10.5/14 in Minion Pro; the display and boxed type is Proxima Nova. Cover designed by Peggy Archambault and interior designed by Delsena Draper. Printed and bound by Versa Press.